Baby Steps of Faith

Hope for Your Adoption Journey

BRENDA MARTIN KOHLBRECHER

ISBN: 978-1-941733-20-2

EA Books, Inc.
eabooksonline.com

SPECIAL THANKS

Thank you God for your faithfulness! The adoption of our daughter Makala and the completion of this devotional testify to your promise of a plan – to give us all hope and a future.

Thanks to my husband Kurt for his commitment to the Lord which has been the bedrock of our marriage. Thanks for always seeing the glass half full. I am forever grateful for the time and space you have given me to explore, dream, and create.

Thanks to my son Kyle, who was but a young boy when these words were penned in my journal. Now, as you graduate college and start your career, I have come to appreciate your tenacity to live out your dreams and it has propelled me to take this book to the finish line.

Thank you Makala, my daughter from South Korea. Without you, there would be no story. Without you, I would have missed the wonder of seeing God work over and over on the adoption journey. Without you my sweet Makala, our family would not be complete.

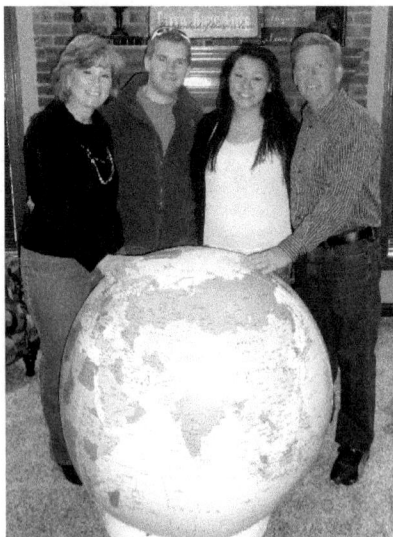

Baby Steps of Faith
Hope for Your Adoption Journey

Brenda Martin Kohlbrecher

Are you thinking about adoption? Perhaps, you have already decided to adopt. Congratulations! This unique devotional was written to inspire, encourage, and strengthen woman dealing with infertility, couples contemplating adoption or currently in the process, and families adopting in response to a child's need for a forever home. Read stories and excerpts penned years ago in the author's adoption journal. Discover how God's Word brought healing, opened her heart, and changed her life. No matter where you are in your walk with God, you can develop a deeper, more intimate relationship with Him. The author invites you to journal your adoption experiences in the interactive resource. Take time to reflect and respond to the *Personal Reflection Questions* on the pages of the interactive journal and spend time in prayer.

Learn how to overcome discouraging obstacles of infertility and inferiority and find freedom. Discover spiritual truths that will equip you to stand and believe, in spite of your fears and doubts, that you were called to adoption. Be encouraged as you endure medical nightmares, paperwork trails, social agency requirements, unexpected news, and delays that result in months – even years – of waiting. The challenges can be numerous and varied when you choose to provide love and a home for an orphan, but never doubt the mighty hand of God. Stretch yourself and your faith to believe that God has a great plan for you and it includes parenthood through adoption. Yes, even if you're single! It just takes *Baby Steps of Faith* to discover God cares about you and the orphans. He has a plan for all of us – to bring hope and a future.

CONTENTS

HOW TO USE THE INTERACTIVE JOURNAL

Congratulations on taking your first step towards becoming a parent through adoption. Children are a wonderful gift; but, I truly believe the real miracle is *how* God brings the children to us. Not everything has to be conventional and I can assure you, God has a plan and purpose for you as a parent. *Baby Steps of Faith – Hope for Your Adoption Journey* will inspire and encourage you.

This devotional book was written from a journal that I penned years ago during my adoption journey. I discovered that keeping a journal was important not only because it documents one's life history, but it can actually be therapeutic and helpful. Journals can be great tools for self-evaluation and self-improvement. We have a tendency to examine our lives a bit more closely when we journal. It can be a safe place to record your deepest thoughts, painful moments, and powerful breakthroughs. These times of reflection can be incredibly beneficial if we are honest and reveal our true self in the responses. Journal your own adoption experiences from beginning to end in this interactive resource.

Each devotional will share a personal story and a scriptural truth. After reading my story, you will spend time reflecting and responding to the *Personal Reflection Question* pertinent to the devotional content. Each *STEP* will ask you to share your situation, apply the scriptural truth, and challenge you to take personal action steps in order to grow. Ultimately, you will discover God's great love for you and call to adoption. It just takes *Baby Steps of Faith.*

HOW TO USE THE INTERACTIVE JOURNAL

S – Share your story: Take time to write your story and compare or contrast to mine. If you have not experienced a particular step in your adoption process because of timing or differing agency procedures, that's alright. Complete it the best you can. Try to stay focused on the key point of the devotional. Meditate on the scriptural truth and let it speak to your heart.

T – Trial or Triumph? It's simple. Give a one answer response. If the experience is difficult or challenging for you, it's a trial, a test. A triumph is the response of one who is not experiencing a challenge in this area, either through practical steps and/or engaging their faith.

E – Explain: Give details in this section. Talk about your weaknesses and insecurities. Open up and share your deepest thoughts and painful moments. On the other hand, share your strengths, your victories, if that's your story. Explain your experiences in detail. Share how your faith or other practical steps have helped you heal or kept this from being a hindrance at all. Be honest and reveal your true self.

P – Personal Action Steps to Grow: The Bible is God's Word to you for teaching, correcting, and training. Listen to the Holy Spirit speak to you through the devotional and the scriptural truth. What is He speaking to your heart? What new truth is being revealed to encourage you or challenge you? Is God asking you to take some action? Listen carefully and respond. The goal of this step is to grow deeper in our relationship with Jesus, to become more like Him in our attitudes and actions, and to learn how to hear God's voice.

S – Supplication: Pray – talk to God about it. Ask God to help you with the trials and give you the strength to make the changes He has revealed to you. Write out specific prayer needs regarding your adoption if pertinent to the devotional topic. Thank Him for the breakthroughs and the blessings. Make your requests known to the Father and pray without ceasing.

Psalm 144:2 He is my loving God and my fortress, my
stronghold and my deliverer, my shield,
in whom I take refuge…

What's your story? Why are you adopting? Are you single,
but have this insatiable desire to be a parent? Maybe you're
married, ready to start a family, and decided to adopt your
first child. Others of you may have large families of home-
grown children, i.e. biological, but have decided there's still
more space in your heart and home. Perhaps, you are facing
issues of infertility and your attempts to have a child, and
start a family, have only resulted in heartache and
disappointment. Whatever the situation, your story has
unfolded nonetheless, and you are adopting.

My story goes like this. I was diagnosed with a large fibroid
tumor embedded in a major uterine artery. After numerous
doctor appointments, including a specialist, it was
determined that a complete hysterectomy was the cure.
Though my world was shaken, I continued to believe God
was still in control…even in the chaos and uncertainty of my
future as a parent. I was devastated that God was aware of
this road I would travel and allowed it to happen; yet, I
knew in order to see the final outcome, I would have to
continue the journey with God. Years later I can tell you that
traveling the adoption road was not easy. I had to begin by
plowing through my new reality, the pain, and oppression. I
continued to heal physically and emotionally while going
through the adoption process. Through it all, I discovered
the same God that David encountered in the Psalms…a
loving God.

I don't know the details of your story or where you're at in the adoption process. If you're hurting, begin to see God as your refuge. Pour your heart out to Him. Share your anger and frustration. He's a big God. He can take it. On the other hand, I pray your adoption experience was not birthed out of a painful time. However, I can assure you, at some point in the adoption process, you will meet adversity and find the need to pour your heart out to the creator of the universe. You'll find that God listens and delivers you - He helps. Adoption takes you through valleys and on top of the mountains…such is life…full of ups and downs. God provides that place of security no matter what you're dealing with in life – He is your fortress. Learn to depend on God. David was running from Saul and hiding in a cave when he wrote this Psalm. He was in desperate need and found only God to be concerned with His situation. David was confident that God would not abandon him – God was his stronghold.

God loves you…values you…and chose you to parent a child through adoption. It's ADOPTION 101 – take refuge in God. Depend and trust Him the very first day of class and every day that follows on your adoption journey.

Baby Steps of Faith Personal Reflection

Psalm 144:2 He is my loving God and my fortress, my
stronghold and my deliverer, my shield,
in whom I take refuge…

Baby Step 1 – What's your story?

Share your Story:

_____

_____

_____

_____

Trial or triumph? _____

Explain:

_____

_____

_____

_____

Personal Action Steps to Grow:

_____

_____

_____

_____

Supplication:

_____

_____

_____

_____

Isaiah 6:8 Then I heard the voice of the LORD saying,
"Whom shall I send? And who will go for us?"

I was 33 years old when I had my hysterectomy. I had one
child – Kyle. I also unexpectedly lost my father to a stroke
just a few months earlier and life seemed to be spiraling out
of control. My husband Kurt and I decided to wait before
making any future decisions regarding adoption. Before I
knew it, two years had come and gone. I continued to work
through the realization of never giving birth to another
child. I was incredibly thankful to have given birth to one
handsome son, but there was a longing in my heart for more
children. I didn't know anything about adoption and the
fear of the unknown was paralyzing. I spent a great deal of
time trying to convince myself *"it's all good"* to quote a
trendy phrase. My life is *"all good."* Any additional time in
my day was spent harboring deep guilt that I wasn't more
grateful and content that I had one child, while others were
completely childless and grieving in ways far beyond my
situation and comprehension. I spent endless hours on this
emotional roller coaster.

My sisters were lifelines during this time. They supported
me in so many ways as I tried to move on after the
hysterectomy. My youngest sister beautifully expressed this
longing as more of a feeling of being incomplete. As I think
back, her comment was more direct, than beautiful, but it's
possible that I may have been a tad bit over sensitive. She
said, "You're just not done yet, that's all, you're just not
done having children." I thought to myself, "What is she

talking about? I had a hysterectomy! The idea of having another child is completely done!" More emphatic than before, she continued, "You and Kurt just need to think about adoption. You're great parents. Kyle would love a brother or sister. It can't hurt to look into it."

From that moment on, thoughts of adoption began to take up head space and I spent many days and nights wrestling with God on the idea. I just wasn't sure it was a good option for us. Are you thinking that same thing? Are you afraid of the unknown? Looking back now, I realize God was gently speaking to me. *"Whom shall I send, and who will go for Me?"* Well, the word choices may not have been quite that eloquent and God did not speak audibly to me, but He began to deposit some thoughts in my mind and they made their way to my heart. There are lots of abandoned, unwanted, orphaned children all over the world. God was asking me to consider meeting a need. Like Isaiah, I heard the Lord say, "Who can I ask to care for them? Will you?" Your current circumstances and this longing you have for a child, could be the beginning of God asking you the very same question.

Baby Steps of Faith Personal Reflection

Isaiah 6:8 Then I heard the voice of the LORD saying, "Whom shall I send? And who will go for us?"

Baby Step 2 – Is God gently speaking to you?

Share your Story:

_____
_____
_____
_____

Trial or triumph? _____

Explain:

_____
_____
_____
_____

Personal Action Steps to Grow:

_____
_____
_____
_____

Supplication:

_____
_____
_____
_____

James 1:27 …look after orphans and widows in their distress
and to keep oneself from being polluted by the world.

God has commanded us to care for the widows and orphans.
He gives them high priority. They are the homeless, the
fatherless, and the motherless. No one calls them sons and
daughters; nor, do the children call out mother or father.
Who's going to care for the orphans? Who will provide a
home? Who will give them a sense of belonging? Could you
be the answer to these questions?

You're reading this devotional, so I believe God sowed the
idea in your heart. He has cultivated, watered, and nurtured
it from the beginning. But will you let it bloom? James warns
us to *keep oneself from being polluted by the world.* How
could our compassion for the orphans become polluted by
the world? I believe this happens when we allow certain
ideas and opinions to invade our minds and hearts…like
these.

**I couldn't love a child that was not my own. I would
have to give birth to a child to feel like they were
really mine.**

**I am not against adopting, but I personally
couldn't handle my child looking different from me.**

**I can't imagine adopting a child from another country.
We've got enough immigrants already.**

**I considered adoption, until I realized the child's
mother could be a prostitute or a drug addict.
I don't feel adoption is right for me.**

**I would love to provide a home to a child,
just not sure a foster-care child...too much baggage.**

These are just a few examples of how the world can pollute
God's command to care for the orphans. Job rescued the
poor, assisted the fatherless, made the widow's heart sing,
and took up the case of a stranger. He put on righteousness
as his clothing. (Job 29) In other words, he did the right thing
in the eyes of God and became an advocate for those who
had no one to speak for them or help them. Jesus
demonstrated this when he said, "Let the little children come
unto me..." because he valued them. They were not a
nuisance and they held a special place in His heart. God
commands us to look after the orphans and to keep our
hearts from being polluted by certain attitudes and critical
thinking. Much like a child is conceived and develops in a
mother's womb, adoption is conceived and grows in a
person's heart. What's bloomin' in your heart?

Baby Steps of Faith Personal Reflection

James 1:27 …look after orphans and widows in their distress
and to keep oneself from being polluted by the world.

Baby Step 3 – Are you being polluted
by the world? Be honest.

Share your Story:

_____
_____
_____
_____

Trial or triumph? _____

Explain:

_____
_____
_____
_____

Personal Action Steps to Grow:

_____
_____
_____
_____

Supplication:

_____
_____
_____
_____

Psalm 127:3-4 Sons are a heritage from the LORD,
children a reward from him. Like arrows in the
hands of a warrior are sons born in one's youth.
Blessed is the man whose quiver is full of them.

Children are a reward from God. Many times I asked this
question, "Lord, where's my reward?" Actually, I had
planned for three rewards. I had one child…a son. Kyle was
a great reward indeed. After attempting to conceive for
eighteen months, his conception and delivery was an
incredible blessing to us. Now he was four and ready for a
sibling. We were ready to add arrows to the quiver, for
"blessed is the man whose quiver is full of them." I
witnessed many over-flowing quivers, leaving my heart full
of discontent, since it wasn't my quiver. How about you?
Friends and family continue to move forward planning
weddings and announcing baby due dates, while you
remain stuck, in this empty place.

It's all but empty. It's a place full of torment,
disappointment, doubt, frustration, and even anger.
Questions run rampant in your mind. Why me? Did I do
something wrong? Is God punishing me? If you're single,
you may have additional noisy questions. Why have I not
found my soul mate? Where's the person God had planned
for me to share my life with and start a family? How does a
single person start a family? Do you find yourself grief
stricken as you lament over all the children you're never
going to have or celebrate? Outwardly, you rejoice with
friends and family in light of their good news, while inside

the battle continues to rage resulting in feelings of hopelessness and despair. Where's my reward God...my heritage? Why have you forgotten me? Why do I feel cursed? I certainly don't feel blessed.

The first verse of Psalm 127 reads "Unless the Lord builds the house, they labor in vain who build it..." We may be able to physically build our homes, choose our spouse, dream of a family, finish school, establish a career; but, how we choose and what we build on will never satisfy us if God is not the foundation. We will labor in vain. God wants to be at the center of our lives. He wants to be the foundation of our life and our partner in life. He desires to be a part of every detail...that includes the blessing of children. God is interested in the details of your life...big and small...including your quiver. Believing this truth is the beginning of an exciting journey with Him.

Baby Steps of Faith Personal Reflection

Psalm 127:3-4 Sons are a heritage from the LORD, children a reward from him. Like arrows in the hands of a warrior are sons born in one's youth. Blessed is the man whose quiver is full of them.

Baby Step 4 – Where's my reward God?

Share your Story:

_____
_____
_____
_____

Trial or triumph? _____

Explain:

_____
_____
_____
_____

Personal Action Steps to Grow:

_____
_____
_____
_____

Supplication:

_____
_____
_____
_____

Jeremiah 29:11 "For I know the plans I have for you,"
declares the LORD, "plans to prosper you and not
to harm you, plans to give you hope and a future."

Why would a loving God grant children to *them* and not
me? I wrestled with this question on more than one occasion
during my recovery and during the adoption process. I had
a difficult time gaining a healthy perspective when it came
to *them* and I would find myself growing increasingly
frustrated and angry. In all honesty, I wasn't just frustrated
at *them*, I was angry and frustrated with God.

You know *them*. Those individuals that emphatically tell
their children they wish they'd never been born. People who
abandon their babies in dumpsters. What's wrong with
them? Every day, children are born into the homes of *them*
who suffer addictions and abuse and become victims of this
tragic behavior. Why *them* God and not me? How come you
gave children to *them* and not me? All of us have a deep
desire to provide loving homes to children…to be parents;
yet, we are childless. What a paradox.

Deep inside, I know God has a plan for me; but I am
confused and broken-hearted at this point in my life because
this plan clearly did not fulfill all my hopes and dreams.
Bitterness had become the root of my anger and frustration.
It was time to get a new attitude…a new perspective. I had
to stop asking the question," Why *them* God and not me?
Unfortunate things happen in life – it's not always fair. I
needed a new set of questions. What can I do to help *them?*
How can I make a difference in these situations and

13

ultimately bring hope to all of us? These children are innocent. The parents need help. In many cases, God needs loving homes for the children he gave to *them.* All of us fall short in life. (Romans 3:23) I decided to be part of the solution, not the problem.

God had a plan for Jeremiah and I was determined to see that same plan fulfilled in my life. The scripture says it's a good and prosperous plan. It was never meant to harm me or hurt me in any way; but, to give me hope and a future. Although my situation appeared hopeless and my future looked grim, I had to trust that God would fulfill these promises in my life. I encourage you today to focus on these truths in God's plan for you. To celebrate and continue this adoption journey with heighten anticipation of what God is planning to do for you. Make a choice today to surrender all your frustration, anger and confusion about *them* to Jesus. Choose to be part of the solution, not the problem. Forgive *them*, ask God to renew your heart, and give you the strength to move forward and not harbor bitterness towards *them.* Let's not waste another day in this sorrowful camp. Let's thank God for his plan and look forward to the future he has for us…all of us. He promises a future full of hope.

Baby Steps of Faith Personal Reflection

Jeremiah 29:11 "For I know the plans I have for you,"
declares the LORD, "plans to prosper you and not
to harm you, plans to give you hope and a future."

Baby Step 5 – Why them God and not me?

Share your Story:

_____
_____
_____
_____

Trial or triumph? _____

Explain:

_____
_____
_____
_____

Personal Action Steps to Grow:

_____
_____
_____
_____

Supplication:

_____
_____
_____
_____

2 Corinthians 4:8-9, 16 We are hard pressed on every side, but not crushed; perplexed, but not in despair; persecuted, but not abandoned; struck down, but not destroyed. Therefore, we do not lose heart.

Being unable to conceive a child is extremely painful and disappointing. It's a valley full of heartache and disappointment that runs deep and wide. You feel hard pressed on every side and perplexed. I was so confused when I received my diagnosis and realized I would never have another child. Do you recognize this valley? Are you walking through it right now? For those of you who have miscarried, your valley includes the sting of death. You know the feeling of being struck down. Parents of adoption endure many days in the valley and a gamut of emotions walking through it. Like Paul, we must come to understand God's sovereign design for affliction. Paul did not enjoy or glorify in affliction, but if he was to undergo suffering, he was determined to endure and have a greater revelation of Jesus when he got to the other side of his pain.

Journal Entry – 1994 Oh, how I long to be pregnant. Sometimes I am just crushed by the reality that my body is unable to bare another child…the miracle of life. At times, I hurt so deep inside myself…never to feel another child in my womb…barren. I know – I've given birth to one child and that is more than many. I am truly grateful; yet, guilt and shame cloud my days of desire for more children. God, please forgive me for yearning to give birth again. I feel so sad and alone – restless. I am confused. Day and night it consumes my thoughts. I don't understand why.

I miss the experience of doctor visits, heart beats, measurements, ultra-sounds, family bets on the sex of the child…boy or girl? I wish I could take back every time I complained about gaining weight at my OBGYN appointments years ago. I would give anything to have those moments again. I miss the milestones to delivery…3 months, 6 months, almost time…9 months…finish line in sight. I long for the excitement of family and friends anxiously awaiting the baby arrival…baby showers. I miss those sweet gifts and surprises from my husband to remind me of his love and pride as I carry our child. Oh, it hurts so deeply. I feel so empty.

Do not lose heart in your valley. Your valley situation may be different than mine, but you are no stranger to pain and disappointment. You can relate to the confusion, restlessness, and brokenness. The only way to get through your valley is to keep moving forward. Reflect on your life. Recall other times when you thought – I AM NOT GOING TO MAKE IT – but you made it through. You are not alone. God is with you. Press through it and keep your eyes on Jesus. For the joy set before Him, Christ endured the cross. (Hebrews 12:2) You will experience a greater revelation of Jesus on the other side of this suffering. His love for you is deeper and wider than your pain. That love and grace will see you through. Do not lose heart – ask God to give you peace and strength for the journey. Be determined – a child is counting on you.

Baby Steps of Faith Personal Reflection

2 Corinthians 4:8-9, 16 We are hard pressed on every side, but not crushed; perplexed, but not in despair; persecuted, but not abandoned; struck down, but not destroyed. Therefore, we do not lose heart.

Baby Step 6 – Are you in a valley?

Share your Story:

_____
_____
_____
_____

Trial or triumph? _____

Explain:

_____
_____
_____
_____

Personal Action Steps to Grow:

_____
_____
_____
_____

Supplication:

_____
_____
_____
_____

Hebrews 11:6 And without faith it is impossible to
please God, because anyone who comes to him
must believe that he exists and that he rewards
those who earnestly seek him.

Life can be unpredictable. I was confident that I would beat
the odds medically and be able to conceive a child again.
But, life threw a curve ball and I had to accept reality. I was
having a complete hysterectomy and I would not bare
anymore children. What's your curve ball? Did life bring a
harsh reality to your doorstep? I prayed night and day
asking God to heal my body, but the tumor remained. I
prayed for God to provide wisdom to the doctors and save
my uterus, but they were not able. No help had come. All
that I had once rested on, believed, and found strength in,
seemed to be crumbling around me. I was losing faith. I had
come to a place where God was no different than man. I
couldn't count on Him. Now what? I wasn't sure what to do
next. I was in a faith crisis. I had to accept that it was God's
will for my life even if I didn't understand it all. I had
resolved to move forward with God in the midst of my
hopelessness. God was sovereign and in control of my life. I
could not lose faith.

Faith matters. Webster defines faith: believing in God or in
God's promises. First, we have to believe in God in order to
have faith. I also believe faith sees the unseen. God is
unseen, but I still believe He exists and I make it my life's
mission to know Him and His will for my life. God is
looking for people who will believe in every situation life

brings. God is looking for people to trust him and his promises when life is going smoothly and when life throws a curveball.

I learned that faith is the human response to God's sovereign power. Faith is believing no matter what takes place in your life that God is still at the helm and all of His promises will not let go of you in the midst of the storm. There will come times when you will not understand and be perplexed. God's thoughts are higher than our thoughts. His ways are not our ways. (Isaiah 55:8) I often say to friends and family when facing senseless times, "I know what it looks like, I'm looking right at it…living it every day; but, I'm trying to see it with eyes of faith." For we walk by faith, not by sight. (2 Corinthians 5:7) How will you respond? Trust God's vision with your reality. Don't be troubled by perplexing times – when you don't understand what God is doing. He still loves you no matter what has happened. I don't know if you have a relationship with God; but, I want you to know that God is interested in your life and loves you right where you're at. Without faith, it's impossible to please God. I weathered my faith crisis. I held on and continued to earnestly seek my God. He rescued me and rewarded me with a beautiful child through adoption. Trust God's ability to bring you through – hold on tight and keep believing. Faith matters.

Baby Steps of Faith Personal Reflection

Hebrews 11:6 And without faith it is impossible to please God, because anyone who comes to him must believe that he exists and that he rewards those who earnestly seek him.

Baby Step 7 – Where's your faith?

Share your Story:

_____

_____

_____

_____

Trial or triumph? _____

Explain:

_____

_____

_____

_____

Personal Action Steps to Grow:

_____

_____

_____

_____

Supplication:

_____

_____

_____

_____

Romans 8:28 And we know that in all things God works for the good of those who love him, who have been called according to his purpose.

Days turned into weeks, into months, and I continued to heal from the surgery. I would awaken early in the morning to face my reality and whisper these words, "God works all things good." Those quiet whispers usually turned to pleading by the time my morning eggs were ready for consumption. I would plead with Him to show me the *good* in the events that just transpired in my life. I certainly didn't see the *good* in having my dreams of more children utterly shattered. All I had remaining in my heart was a tiny mustard seed of faith. (Matthew 17:20)

How is God going to make this *good*? How can this tragic event in my life become favorable? Romans 8:28 tells us that God desires *to work all things good for those who love him and for those who have been called* according to His purpose. Those are two important conditions; otherwise, I have found that suffering itself is not beneficial. If we dwell on our situation and our pain, we never gain a higher perspective. But if we focus on what God can do through our suffering and continue to love Him, we will find strength, perseverance, and hope. I started to find some good when I shifted my focus to God and allowed Him to work in me and my situation.

"Called according to God's purpose" – God's calling is simply his personal invitation to carry out the unique task

He has for you. But, before you can discover God's calling, you must believe in God and His Only Son, Jesus Christ. Let me tell you my friend, faith in God and a love relationship with His Son, Jesus, is more important than any other single factor in your life. Make the decision to follow Jesus. Accept His personal salvation. Let Him lead your life and help you carry out the unique task He has for you – to adopt a child. I believe this is your calling. Take Him along on your journey. Get ready for Jesus to reveal Himself through your adoption experience. You will never regret it. You'll be glad He came!

Baby Steps of Faith Personal Reflection

Romans 8:28 And we know that in all things God works for the good of those who love him, who have been called according to his purpose.

Baby Step 8 – Is God calling you?

Share your Story:

_____
_____
_____
_____

Trial or triumph? _____

Explain:

_____
_____
_____
_____

Personal Action Steps to Grow:

_____
_____
_____
_____

Supplication:

_____
_____
_____
_____

Deuteronomy 30:19-20 Now choose life, so that you and
your children may live and that you may love the
LORD your God, listen to his voice and hold
fast to him. For the LORD is your life…

Choices – life is full of choices. Once we made the decision to
adopt, we were overwhelmed with more choices. Would
you like to pursue a domestic or international adoption? Are
you considering an open or closed adoption? Are you
wanting to adopt a newborn of your race/ethnic
background or would you consider a blended family? Do
you see yourself adopting a special needs child? Get the
picture? You will have so many decisions to make. I want to
encourage you once again to choose Jesus first. He will fill
you with wisdom and guide you on this amazing adoption
journey. If you already have a relationship with Jesus, that's
wonderful. I celebrate with you. But, if you haven't accepted
Christ, it's not too late.

When God created man He created us with our *free will*
which enables us to *make choices in life*. For every choice we
make there is a reward or a consequence. He created the first
man and woman, Adam and Eve. Let me tell you more
about the choice they made, which had serious consequences
for all of mankind. God's plan in creating Adam and Eve
was perfect fellowship in a perfect world. There was no
selfishness, sadness or death in this beautiful world God
created for these two people. Everything in the garden was
for their enjoyment except for the fruit on the tree of
knowledge. But Adam and Eve disobeyed God and ate the

forbidden fruit and everything fell apart. Since then, every person born, is born a sinner. Our sin separates us from God. If we stay in this condition, we will be eternally separated from God in a place called hell.

That was never God's plan. To fix Adam's poor choice, God sent Jesus to earth to try and get us back to following the original plan. God wants to reconcile each of us. Sin entered our world through Adam and Eve's disobedience and rebellion. Reconciliation entered the world through Jesus' death on the cross and His resurrection. However, salvation will only enter your life when you acknowledge what Jesus did to pay your debt for sin and rebellion and accept His sacrifice for you. No one can do this for you. It's your choice. God gave each of us a free will and only you can chose to walk in His plan or your own. I pray you choose to follow Jesus and allow Him to lavish His great love on you, to guide you all the days of your life, and at this crucial time, trust Him to fulfill the calling on your life to adopt.

Baby Steps of Faith Personal Reflection

Deuteronomy 30:19-20 Now choose life, so that you and
your children may live and that you may love the
LORD your God, listen to his voice and hold
fast to him. For the LORD is your life...

Baby Step 9 – Do you want to choose Jesus?

Share your Story:

_____
_____
_____
_____

Trial or triumph? _____

Explain:

_____
_____
_____
_____

Personal Action Steps to Grow:

_____
_____
_____
_____

Supplication:

_____
_____
_____
_____

John 1:12 Yet to all who received him, to those who
believed in his name (Jesus), he gave the right to
become children of God.

We want to give our adopted children hope and a future.
God wants to do the same thing for you. Accept Jesus Christ
as your Lord and Savior. Make a decision right now to
profess your faith in God and receive Jesus Christ in your
heart. Believe today that He is the Son of the living God.
Believe today that He came down from heaven as the Savior
of the world, died on a cross for your sins, rose from the
dead, and ascended into heaven. He did it all for you and
me, so that we might be *adopted* into the family of God.

My name is _____.

_____ Yes, I want to profess my faith in God and receive
Jesus as my Savior.

Recite this prayer to your heavenly Father:

Lord God, I realize now that I am a sinner. Forgive me
Father. Cleanse me from all unrighteousness. I want to be
adopted into your heavenly family. I thank you for the
opportunity you have given to me as I profess my faith in
Jesus, your Son. I believe in you Jesus. I believe you came to
earth, died on a cross for my sin, was buried, and rose again
three days later. Come and live in my heart. Help me to live
for you and serve you all the days of my life. I love you.
Amen.

On this day, _____, I
made my decision to follow Christ. I look forward to
growing my relationship with God and Jesus through
reading the Bible, prayer, and worship. I am thankful for
their love and forgiveness. I am so blessed to be a part of
God's **adopted** family. I am so grateful that He has a plan for
my life, including this adoption journey. Thank you Father
God.

Congratulations! Welcome to the family of God!

Baby Steps of Faith Personal Reflection

John 1:12 Yet to all who received him, to those who
believed in his name (Jesus), he gave the right to
become children of God.

Baby Step 10 – Share your story adopted child of God!

Share your Story:

_____
_____
_____
_____

Trial or triumph? _____

Explain:

_____
_____
_____
_____

Personal Action Steps to Grow:

_____
_____
_____
_____

Supplication:

_____
_____
_____
_____

Romans 8:14-15 Because those who are led by the
Spirit of God are sons of God. For you did not
receive a spirit that makes you a slave again to
fear, but you received the Spirit of sonship."

I accepted Christ when I was nineteen years old. He is my
best friend and I love Him with all my heart. I can't imagine
life without Him. He calls me daughter and I call Him Father
God. I am a child of the Most High God. It's an
overwhelming thought.

In your decision to accept Christ, you were adopted into
God's family. Your life will never be the same. You could
not ask for a better Father – than God. Get ready for the
adventure of a lifetime! Read the Bible so that you may come
to a deeper understanding of who God is and His Son Jesus.
Memorize scripture and let it renew your heart and
transform your mind. Talk with God daily through prayer
and by meditating on the scriptures. Find a good bible-
teaching church and worship the Lord. Fellowship with
other Christians weekly – they will build you up and
encourage you to live for Jesus and be like Him. God
believes in you. He loves and cares for you. You are His
child. Here's what He has to say about you. Read these daily
to build your faith and to remind yourself of God's great
love for you.

YOU ARE...

- A child of God (Romans 8:16)
- Redeemed from the hand of the enemy (Psalm 107:2)

- Forgiven (Colossians 1:13-14)
- Saved by Grace through Faith (Ephesians 2:8)
- Justified (Romans 5:1)
- Sanctified (1 Corinthians 6:11)
- A New Creature (2 Corinthians 5:17)
- Partaker of His Divine Nature (2 Peter 1:4)
- Redeemed from the Curse of the Law (Galatians 3:13)
- Delivered from the Powers of Darkness (Colossians 1:13)
- Led by the Spirit of God (Romans 8:14)
- A Son of God (Romans 8:14)
- Kept in Safety wherever I go (Psalm 91:1)
- Getting all my needs met by Jesus (Philippians 4:19)
- Casting all my cares upon Jesus (1Peter 5:7)
- Strong in the Lord and in His might (Ephesians 6:10)
- Doing all things through Christ who strengthens me (Philippians 4:13)
- An Heir of God/Joint Heir with Jesus (Romans 8:17)

Baby Steps of Faith Personal Reflection

Romans 8:14-15 Because those who are led by the
Spirit of God are sons of God. For you did not
receive a spirit that makes you a slave again to
fear, but you received the Spirit of sonship."

Baby Step 11 – Which one on the list overwhelms you?

Share your Story:

_____
_____
_____
_____

Trial or triumph? _____

Explain:

_____
_____
_____
_____

Personal Action Steps to Grow:

_____
_____
_____
_____

Supplication:

_____
_____
_____
_____

Isaiah 43:18-19 Forget the former things; do not dwell
on the past. See, I am doing a new thing! Now it
springs up; do you not perceive it? I am making
a way in the desert and streams in the wasteland.

Have you ever had the experience of being introduced to an
unfamiliar word while reading or watching a television
program? You're intrigued by the word and grab a
dictionary to see what it means. Suddenly, you hear *that
word* and see it constantly. This strange phenomenon can
also take place with familiar words. All that said, *that word*
– familiar or unfamiliar – invariably comes up many times
throughout your day.

This describes what happened to us and the adoption
process. Adoption was familiar to us; but, certainly not a
topic of discussion or a word regularly spoken in our
household. We never talked about it, read about it, or
thought about it. My husband and I only knew two couples
who had adopted children. Now, without trying, *that word
– adoption* permeated our lives. We constantly met adopted
people and people who were adopting. It seemed as if they
were thrown into our daily routines and conversations. Our
senses were heightened and for the first time, we also
noticed the foreign faces that graced the small community
where we lived. Apparently, many of them were adopted.
How is it we never noticed or heard of this before?

Working with the adoption agency definitely opened doors
to meet perspective adoptive couples and new adoptees. It
made perfect sense, that the topic of adoption would be

heard in these circles of conversation, but this was different. It was a spontaneous explosion of *that word – adoption*. It surfaced in conversations with strangers and outside of the adoption agency walls. Over and over again we met people touched by adoption – a waitress in a restaurant, a family met on vacation, and ironically, the substitute teacher who covered my medical leave while I recovered from the hysterectomy.

God continued to bring these special people and powerful stories of adoption into our daily routine. Isaiah 43 tells us when God does a new thing, it springs up. God didn't want us dwelling on the past, He wanted us to forget the former things, and see the new thing he longed to do in our life – adoption. This fresh new thing was like a stream in our desert. Perceive means to be aware of through the senses – to see, hear, taste, smell, or feel. To take in with one's mind – to observe. God was definitely doing a new thing. He was asking, "Do you perceive it? - *Do you see it*? "Yes, we perceive it, Lord! - *Yes, we see it!* Perhaps God is doing a new thing in your life through adoption. Like us, I hope you are hearing and seeing it spring up around you every day. Don't dwell in the past. Give up that desert for a fresh stream of living water.

Baby Steps of Faith Personal Reflection

Isaiah 43:18-19 Forget the former things; do not dwell
on the past. See, I am doing a new thing! Now it
springs up; do you not perceive it? I am making
a way in the desert and streams in the wasteland.

Baby Step 12 – What new thing do you perceive?

Share your Story:

_____
_____
_____
_____

Trial or triumph? _____

Explain:

_____
_____
_____
_____

Personal Action Steps to Grow:

_____
_____
_____
_____

Supplication:

_____
_____
_____
_____

Proverbs 16:9 In his heart a man plans his course,
but the LORD determines his steps.

You've decided to adopt! Where do you start? We started by contacting adoption agencies. Packets began to arrive in the mail and it didn't take long to create piles of paperwork. The calendar filled up with adoption seminars and domestic workshops. If you choose domestic adoption, you will adopt within the U.S. That invited the possibility of meeting the birth mother creating a special, unsettling and awkward situation all at once. She could change her mind. Plus a relevant search for the biological father was mandatory. It provided an opportunity for him to relinquish his rights to the child. This is vitally important and prevents the possibility of his attempting to attain custody of the adopted child at a later time. However, he could choose to keep the child once he learned he was a father. Does that make you nervous?

Meetings with adoption attorneys and international workshops were scheduled. International adoptions involve adopting a child from another country. Prepare to travel. It could be a long journey and over the ocean. It's helpful if you speak a foreign language, but an interpreter is available in most cases. One other detail – it's imperative that you know the location of the nearest U.S. embassy in case there would be an international incident. Does that scare you?

For the record, domestic and international adoptions often require a psychological evaluation. There's also required cultural training when seeking to adopt a foreign child. Are you ready to learn more about your child's culture and how to incorporate it into your daily routine? Does that overwhelm you?

Phone calls were made to various social-service agencies to become educated on foster-care procedures and adoption placements. Foster care places a child into your home, once you become a state-certified caregiver – a foster parent. You become responsible for the day-to-day care of a child, but there are no guarantees that you will adopt the child placed within your home. Does that disappoint you?

Which way do you go? It's a big decision and unchartered territory for most of us. God led me to Proverbs during this time. "Make a decision (make plans) and He will establish it (order your steps). Our lives unfold line by line like a novel. Your adoption will do the same. God is the Author and Finisher of both. There will be uncertain times – twists and turns in the plot, and scary places. That's not easy for us because we're human and predisposed to fear and doubt. Be strong and courageous, God directs your steps and it's a wonderful thing to be directed by God. He will take whatever's bad and transform it, turning you and your situation around. No matter what our journeys lead us through, we always end up in God. It's a heavenly adoption voyage – make a decision and rest in Him for the outcome. He has your best interest at heart.

Baby Steps of Faith Personal Reflection

Proverbs 16:9 In his heart a man plans his course,
but the LORD determines his steps.

Baby Step 13 – Which way are you going?

Share your Story:

_____

_____

_____

_____

Trial or triumph? _____

Explain:

_____

_____

_____

_____

Personal Action Steps to Grow:

_____

_____

_____

_____

Supplication:

_____

_____

_____

_____

Deuteronomy 31:8 The LORD Himself goes before you
and will be with you…do not be afraid;
do not be discouraged.

Adopting a child is a big decision. There's many different
avenues to take: domestic, international, foster care, placing
a file with an adoption attorney, or creating a family
portfolio to be placed in a charitable home for unwed
mothers who choose a family for their unborn child – via the
portfolio information.

That's more than enough; yet, we had an entirely new set of
adoption decisions to think about, iron out, and fret over.
Perhaps like us you have children, but desire more. Who
will care for your current children while you're traveling
across the country? How will adding to your family through
adoption affect the children you have already? We
considered having our child travel with us, but the agency
advised us not to for various reasons. On top of that, the
agency recommended special immunizations, when
traveling abroad to remote areas, in order to avoid disease
and parasites. I had nightmares of our son announcing to
everyone, "My parents died in a fatal accident or contracted
a deadly disease because they traveled across the world to
adopt a sibling, so that I would not grow up an *only* child!" I
started to panic about our decision to adopt, even though I
knew it was God's will for us.

Growing up as a child, I remember riding a bicycle built for
two. It was scary when you weren't riding up front and
steering the bike. Taking on speed down a hill and turning

corners always seemed much faster and closer to the edge when I couldn't steer the bike. I was totally dependent on the driver up front, who had full control. Sometimes I would panic and drag my feet to slow the bike down or scream, "Stop!" My reaction is similar when I'm following God's will and suddenly meet daunting circumstances. Sometimes I follow my heavenly Father with total assurance until the way gets rough, the terrain gets steep. Often times I begin to question the Lord. Can He not see the threats, the danger, the uncertainty of this path? I find I want to drag my feet or turn back. Ever feel that way?

God knows what is before us. We get frightened because we're looking at the danger rather than resting in the promise of His faithfulness. He has a destination in mind, just like the lead rider on that bicycle built for two. God knows where you're going on this adoption road…just like He lead Moses, and Joshua and the people of Israel. They didn't need to fear. Let's focus on the fact that God goes before us and with us. Enjoy the ride.

Baby Steps of Faith Personal Reflection

Deuteronomy 31:8 The LORD Himself goes before you
and will be with you…do not be afraid;
do not be discouraged.

Baby Step 14 – What's pushing your panic button?

Share your Story:
_____
_____
_____
_____

Trial or triumph? _____
Explain:
_____
_____
_____
_____

Personal Action Steps to Grow:
_____
_____
_____
_____

Supplication:
_____
_____
_____
_____

Isaiah 48:17 I am the LORD your God, who teaches
you what is best for you, who directs you in the
way you should go.

I remember the day we decided to adopt international.
Obviously, we conquered our fear of traveling over the
ocean. Once we declared international, it was time to select
one of the countries represented by our adoption agency.
China? Korea? Philippines? *This* decision was going to be
easy. It was simply the answer to one important question.
Which country can deliver a child to us the fastest? Korea
appeared to be the logical choice with a wait time of
eighteen months from the beginning of the process to the
child's arrival. That was two gestational cycles. I found that
more than manageable. There was so much to be done and I
was certain that eighteen months would go by quickly. The
agency encouraged us to get started immediately, and
assured us that before we knew it, our name would be at the
top of the list for the next available Korean child needing a
forever home.

Then we met a family who received their child in six months
and everything changed. They had adopted from the
Philippines. There was no wait time. The placement of a
child, simply hinged on your family being matched to a
child by the Filipino Social Services. There were no
guarantees on the time frame of that decision, but we
decided to take a chance. It was a gamble. Deep down
inside, I believed the odds were in our favor. I believed we
walked in God's favor. We had so much love to give, a

strong marriage, a little brother, excited extended family...what's not to love about us, right? God revealed this scripture to me later that day in my quiet time. Isaiah 48:17 "I am the Lord your God, who teaches you what is best for you, who directs you in the way you should go."

Our adoption journey was about to begin. God turned my "gambling" instinct into a constructive force. My journey would include challenging the winds, scaling the heights, walking through valleys and climbing mountains. Are you encountering any of these on your adoption journey?

The adoption process turned out to be incredibly long and difficult. It was anything but quick and easy. Is your journey long and difficult? Some translations state, "I am the Lord your God, who teaches you to profit. Profit is something gained or benefited in doing something. Those challenging winds, valleys, and mountains were not easy at the time. I didn't think God was doing me any favors. I didn't believe God's favor was with us at all, but God was making me strong and building my faith. In time, I learned first-hand that God does go before me and His awesome hand of blessing does in fact rest on my head. Maybe things aren't going exactly as you had planned either, but trust that God knows what's best for you and the road your traveling is exactly where he wanted you to go. God's favor and hand of blessing are on your adoption.

Baby Steps of Faith Personal Reflection

Isaiah 48:17 I am the LORD your God, who teaches
you what is best for you, who directs you in the
way you should go.

Baby Step 15 – What tough lesson is God teaching you?

Share your Story:

_____
_____
_____
_____

Trial or triumph? _____

Explain:

_____
_____
_____
_____

Personal Action Steps to Grow:

_____
_____
_____
_____

Supplication:

_____
_____
_____
_____

Isaiah 40:31 But those who hope in the LORD will
renew their strength. They will soar on wings
of eagles; they will run and not grow weary,
they will walk and not be faint.

God allowed us to wait on our adoption journey. I didn't
like it much. Fortunately, He renewed my strength daily,
picked me up when I was down, and believed that I could
complete the task of becoming a parent of adoption. I
learned to wait for a child, but more than anything, I learned
to *wait on God* through the adoption process.

These inspirational words from Isaiah do inspire us with
results; but, they are conditional. Renewed strength,
mounting with wings of eagles, and running without
fainting only come when you wait upon the Lord. I would
like to think I have improved at waiting on God's timing in
other areas of my life, as my relationship with Him has
grown over the years, but I still find it challenging and even
a bit perplexing. Why does God answer some of my prayers
quickly; yet, other times I still have to wait? I think it's even
more difficult today because we live in a century that's
moving incredibly fast. Technology has enabled us to multi-
task and get answers quickly…just Google it! We have
instant coffee, fast-food, email…we don't wait too long for
anything and that doesn't help us to exercise patience in our
personal situations.

I know God hears my prayers and at times allows the wait.
God, in His infinite wisdom, knows how to use time. He is a
gentle teacher. It's during the waiting times that He builds

character in us and tests our faith. I also believe **God is waiting**. He is waiting on us to finish our assignments. His lessons can be challenging and sometimes we sit in the classroom of teaching for a long time. Sometimes we have to repeat a lesson. Just ask the Israelites. They spent forty years going around the same mountain in the same place because they didn't listen to God's instructions. Can you relate? My course went on for two years, with lessons repeated and tested constantly. Perhaps, that's why this verse has become my life verse – that is a single scripture that has encouraged me over and over again in my life.

In spite of the hard lessons and difficult tests, I would learn to love my teacher, Jesus. I discovered the lessons and tests were beneficial. Now, when my prayers are delayed, I immediately ask God if He's trying to teach me something. I sit still (wait upon the Lord). I sharpen my pencil and listen to instruction (renew my strength). Next, I apply what I have learned (mount with wings of an eagle) and pass the test quickly as possible (run and not be weary) and endure to the finish line.

Baby Steps of Faith Personal Reflection

Isaiah 40:31 But those who hope in the LORD will
renew their strength. They will soar on wings
of eagles; they will run and not grow weary,
they will walk and not be faint.

Baby Step 16 – Is God waiting on you to finish an assignment?

Share your Story:

_____
_____
_____
_____

Trial or triumph? _____

Explain:

_____
_____
_____
_____

Personal Action Steps to Grow:

_____
_____
_____
_____

Supplication:

_____
_____
_____
_____

Isaiah 65:24 Before they call I will answer;
while they are still speaking I will hear.

Kyle Allan was born to the Kohlbrecher quiver December 17, 1990. We call Kyle "home-grown" since I gave birth to this handsome child. People chuckle when we announce that Kyle is our domestic and Makala is our import. Kyle's birth is an amazing story. A story that demonstrates God's faithfulness. Nothing is coincidental in the life of a Christian. God is about everything in our lives. I share this story with you to inspire you to continue to believe in your plan for a child to unfold.

We had been trying to have a baby for about eighteen months. We prayed and prayed, but still no baby news to share. One Sunday we attended service at a church we had visited a few times. There were familiar faces in the congregation; but most were new to my husband and me. The worship and message were wonderful. God's presence was strong in the service.

At the end of the message, the pastor invited anyone needing prayer to come forward. Without hesitation, we went to the altar. My heart was discouraged in our failed attempts to get pregnant. I welcomed the prayer. There were several people who went forward and lines began to form. The pastor and a few other leaders were praying over people one by one. We were next in line. One of the leaders smiled and motioned for us to step forward.

We had never met and no words were spoken about our need. She gently rested her hands on us both and began to pray. She stopped mid-way through her prayer, tilted her head, looked into our eyes, and asked, "Are you trying to have a baby?" Of course, we were so moved and amazed that she knew our need without so much as a spoken word, that we began to cry. We could barely mutter the word "yes" and nodded our heads in response. She smiled, leaned in closely to both of us, and said with great delight, "You're already pregnant." Needless to say, we were shocked and surprised by her words. She spoke with such confidence and assurance. Her great faith moved us and challenged us at the same time. Could she be right? How did she know? Did God tell her this?

A few weeks later it was confirmed. I was indeed pregnant. This gifted prayer warrior was able to deliver that message because she was confident in God and what He had revealed to her by His spirit. He is a mighty God in "that before they call, I will answer; And while they are still speaking, I will hear." He answered our prayers. It was done. I hope this story stirs great faith in you to be confident that your prayer for a child will be answered. God hears.

Baby Steps of Faith Personal Reflection

Isaiah 65:24 Before they call I will answer;
while they are still speaking I will hear.

Baby Step 17 – Any recent answer to prayer?

Share your Story:

_____
_____
_____
_____

Trial or triumph? _____

Explain:

_____
_____
_____
_____

Personal Action Steps to Grow:

_____
_____
_____
_____

Supplication:

_____
_____
_____
_____

Proverbs 23:7 For he is the kind of man who is always
thinking about the costs…but his heart is not
with you.

Adoption requires a homestudy. A homestudy is basically a
written report completed by your social worker who
investigates the health, medical, criminal, family, and
backgrounds of adoptive parents. In short, our job was to
complete mounds of paperwork and answer tons of
questions. A large portion of this process includes examining
one's personal history - childhood, parental relationships,
interactions with siblings, your home life and more. The
agency examines your parenting ideas, how you plan to
establish a family through adoption, and your abilities to
provide the needs of a child. The home-study helps the
courts and the adoption agency to determine whether you
are qualified to adopt.

No pressure, right? Immediately, I began to recollect each of
my failures in life, shortcomings, and every negative
comment that reinforced what I thought about myself. I
couldn't help but dwell on all my weaknesses which led to
all my insecurities and inferiorities kicking into overdrive.
Please do not make me examine every detail of my life, tell
you about it, and remain confident that I will qualify for
anything. Proverbs 23:7 teaches us that we become what we
think in our hearts. Many times we believe things about
ourselves that aren't true at all. We believe we have little or
no value, feel worthless, and can't seem to measure up to
everyone else. Every hurt, negative comment, failure, and

insecurity will determine what we think about ourselves if we let it.

Our minds are like computers. They know nothing except what they have been fed. And, like a computer, our mind can be affected by bad data and viruses. Clearly I needed some antivirus software. I needed to meditate on the Word of God. It's up to us to make the change in our thinking by reading and digesting God's Word. We can control what we dwell on. Even though God's plan is good, you must believe it to receive it and then confess it. We can slow down the plan of God by what we think. As followers of Jesus, we are to be thinking on what is true, honest, just, pure, lovely, of good report, virtuous, and praiseworthy. (Phil 4:8) God says I am a masterpiece, fearfully and wonderfully made, chosen to be a part of His family, and called to adoption. It's an important assignment. Sharpen your pencil or charge up that laptop and answer each homestudy question knowing you are qualified by the One who called you.

Baby Steps of Faith Personal Reflection

Proverbs 23:7 For he is the kind of man who is always
thinking about the costs…but his heart is not
with you.

Baby Step 18 – What negative thinking is holding you back?

Share your Story:

_____
_____
_____
_____

Trial or triumph? _____

Explain:

_____
_____
_____
_____

Personal Action Steps to Grow:

_____
_____
_____
_____

Supplication:

_____
_____
_____
_____

Genesis 9:13 I have set my rainbow in the clouds, and it will
be the sign of the covenant between me and earth.

One late afternoon my husband surprised me with an
invitation to dine out for the evening. It was a simple gesture
to lift my spirits as we waited for the adoption agency to
complete the initial homestudy review and accept us as
parents of adoption. A spring storm was brewing, so we
ventured close to home. As I watched the storm build across
the open skies, I couldn't help but see the symbolism
between it and my life. The wind was blowing strong and
the tree branches tossed to and fro. That is exactly how we
often respond to trials and hardships. The rain rolling down
the windows, caused me to recall the scripture – tears have
been my food day and night. (Psalm 42:3) I prayed all the
time – rattling the gates of heaven. Picture it, my hands
gripping the gate, white knuckled, shaking the metal bars,
sweat on my brow, fear stricken and shouting, "Jesus, are
you in there? Oh God, please let this agency find us worthy
of parenting and give me another child." They were
desperate prayers full of fear, not faith.

Three months had gone by. How would I ever endure
waiting a year or two for a child? The waters were rising in
this wait. I was drowning in this flood of emotions. I was
miles away in my thoughts as we sat in the restaurant, when
my husband pulled out a large envelope that captured my
attention. There was no postage or return address. It simply
had our name hand-written across the front. I opened it and
quickly recognized that familiar big bundle of paperwork. It

was the homestudy. The review was finished and ready for our final reading, approval and signature. Sitting side by side, we began reading every word of the caseworker's observations. With tremendous relief, we noted the agency's final decision – qualified – approved.

Suddenly, we noticed the restaurant patrons moving towards the windows. Apparently, the sun began to break through the ominous storm clouds and there in all its glory, was a breath-taking rainbow. Did you know the darker the storm clouds, the brighter the rainbow?

I believe that is symbolic of God's mercy and grace in our situations. His light breaks forth and changes our dark condition. No matter what the trial, His plan is carefully at work to reveal His glory. The rainbow is a reminder of the character of God and our relationship to Him. God comes to us with promises, not demands. God is so full of love and grace for us that He makes commitments that are not based on our performance. When we become fearful and overwhelmed by the storms of life, the wind and heavy rains, God shows the seal of His promise. We may fail, but God is faithful. Rainbows have promise and potential. We will *never* be cut off by any further disaster like the flood – *never*. The future is before us. We have God's promise.

Baby Steps of Faith Personal Reflection

Genesis 9:13 I have set my rainbow in the clouds, and it will be the sign of the covenant between me and earth.

Baby Step 19 – Is there a storm brewing?

Share your Story:

_____

_____

_____

_____

Trial or triumph? _____

Explain:

_____

_____

_____

_____

Personal Action Steps to Grow:

_____

_____

_____

_____

Supplication:

_____

_____

_____

_____

Psalm 127:1 Unless the LORD builds the house, its
builders labor in vain.

Adoption Checklist: Homestudy, *notarizations,* signatures,
physicals, cultural trainings, *more notarizations*, legal
documents, fees, *more notarizations*, picture portfolio, state
seals, passports, *more notarizations*, psychological
evaluations, travel plans, and *more notarizations*! Parents of
adoption understand labor. Not even Lamaze could lessen
this labor! Like building a house, there are many steps in the
adoption process and it takes hard work.

It took months to complete the homestudy, the review
process, and qualify within our local adoption agency
Lifelink. That was just the beginning. That massive file
would now become known as our dossier and sent overseas
to the adopting country of our choice – Philippines. It had to
be reviewed and approved by the foreign agency before a
child could be matched to our family.

Completing the steps in the adoption process is like building
a *big house* indeed and the builders build in vain – unless
the Lord builds it. Adoptive parents complete paperwork in
vain – unless the Lord is involved in the process. It doesn't
mean we can't build; but what we build will not last if God
is not involved in it. Work done independently of God will
be in vain and likely produce little success and poor results. I
want to encourage you to see God as your partner in this
building process of completing all the necessary documents
for your adoption and receiving all the approvals you need.

He will give you the ability to do it, wisdom to answer tough questions, strength to complete the task, and favor.

As I mentioned earlier, once we were approved state side, the dossier was sent overseas, because it was an international adoption. A few weeks went by and no word on the final step, the completion of our house…approval overseas. I was glad to know that I had partnered with the Master Builder and that He watches over the work of man. He helped us gather the documents, gave us wisdom, courage, and strength to complete our checklist: home study questions, notarizations, physicals, cultural trainings, state seals, passports. It would not be in vain. It would all be worthwhile and successful because God was supporting our efforts in building this house. With the Lord, your labor will bear much fruit, and your lives will be secure. Believing this truth will help you time and time again on this adoption journey.

Baby Steps of Faith Personal Reflection

Psalm 127:1 Unless the LORD builds the house, its builders labor in vain.

Baby Step 20 – Labor pains, anyone?

Share your Story:

_____
_____
_____
_____

Trial or triumph? _____

Explain:

_____
_____
_____
_____

Personal Action Steps to Grow:

_____
_____
_____
_____

Supplication:

_____
_____
_____
_____

Micah 7:7 But as for me, I watch in hope for the LORD,
I wait for God my Savior, my God will hear me.

Are you expecting? Sure you are. We are all constantly expecting – the weather to change – a raise on the job – our spouses to understand us better – our friends to be there when we need them – the list goes on and on. I learned a valuable lesson about *great expectations* while vacationing with family one Thanksgiving holiday. My sister-in-law had miscarried over the summer and along with the fall season, came the announcement that she was expecting another baby. The pregnancy was experiencing a few bumps which left her incredibly anxious and concerned. She didn't know quite what to expect. Would she carry *this* baby full term?

On one of our shopping trips, I found her spending a great deal of time in the mall bookstore reading medical books in her attempts to gain a greater understanding of what her physical body was experiencing. It was hard not to worry about this new pregnancy; after all, she wasn't expecting a miscarriage earlier that summer. Painful things happen and can burden your heart with a load. It was difficult to hope and wait to see if this pregnancy would go full term and ultimately deliver a healthy baby. I encouraged her to spend less time in the bookstore reading medical books and avoid "nursing" her fears and spend some time looking forward to and actually planning for the new baby. After all, we were in a mall and the goal was shopping!

But as for me, I will watch *expectantly* for the Lord. (NASB) I encouraged her to look to God and find rest in His infinite wisdom regarding the miscarriage and all her questions. The Lord is honest and forthright. He warns us that we will go through trials and tribulations, but He also assures us that He will be there at the end of the day and you can expect a wonderful ending. In my attempt to get her out of the bookstore and shift her focus, I suggested we go purchase something new for the babies we were expecting.

God calls us to expectation – to anticipate, hope, and confidently believe something. He wants us to demonstrate our faith in Him in words and actions. Are you expecting? God is faithful to deliver.

Excerpt from Joyce Meyer – When, God, When? – Waiting is "to expect" or "to look for" and "to serve." Just like a waiter waits on a table in a restaurant...we must serve...we keep moving while we wait. We serve actively, aggressively and expectantly...

Baby Steps of Faith Personal Reflection

Micah 7:7 But as for me, I watch in hope for the LORD,
I wait for God my Savior, my God will hear me.

Baby Step 21 – What keeps you from expecting God to deliver?

Share your Story:

_____
_____
_____
_____

Trial or triumph? _____

Explain:

_____
_____
_____
_____

Personal Action Steps to Grow:

_____
_____
_____
_____

Supplication:

_____
_____
_____
_____

Psalm 37:4 Delight yourself in the LORD, and
he will give you the desires of your heart.

I remember as a child, the delight it brought me to wish
upon a star. I would simply lock eyes on that blazing beauty
shining in the night sky, concentrate intently on the specific
desire, and make a wish. It was exciting and the thought of
my wish actually coming true and from something so
simple, made it so much fun. It was the definition of delight
– something that brings great enjoyment and pleasure. A
wish is defined as a longing for, a want, desire, or request.
I'm not a child anymore; but, there are days when I fail to
trust God, pull out my grown-up wish list, and go star
gazing. I wish God would do this. I wish God would do that.

We're all wishing for something. We all have a need for one
more thing or at least think we do. Maybe you're wishing for
a spouse, a new job, better health, more finances, or a child.
People have longings, desires, and lots of wants. Eventually,
we make our requests known to God and everyone else
who's within a stone's throw. I tell my children, "I know
what you *want*, but I'm fairly sure you don't *need* it." God is
just like that with us, His children. He knows what we want,
but ultimately knows what's best.

Delight yourself in the Lord and He will give you the desires
of your heart. Does this mean God will give us anything we
desire? Not at all - that's not what this scripture implies.
Look carefully, it's conditional. Delight in the Lord. Find
your pleasure and joy in your relationship with God. When
you love God above all else, your desires will become what

He desires for you – what God wants for your life will matter most to you. Let me tell you friend, it means so much more when God gives us something we desire.

Stop wishing and start praying. Present your requests to God. Commit your way to Him. If I had spent more time praying about the adoption and letting God be God in my life, instead of wishing for things and trying to make things happen, I would have struggled less along the way. Wish upon a star? Leave that for fairy tales. I want to encourage you to seek the star's Creator. He wants to give you the desires of your heart.

Baby Steps of Faith Personal Reflection

Psalm 37:4 Delight yourself in the LORD, and
he will give you the desires of your heart.

Baby Step 22 – What's at the top of your prayer list?

Share your Story:

_____
_____
_____
_____

Trial or triumph? _____

Explain:

_____
_____
_____
_____

Personal Action Steps to Grow:

_____
_____
_____
_____

Supplication:

_____
_____
_____
_____

Mark 9:37 Whoever welcomes one of these
little children in my name welcomes me...

Christmas Eve – 1996 – The dossier was approved in the
Philippines! It was officially signed and sealed. The process
took six months, but it seemed like years. It was Christmas
Eve and the house was decorated beautifully – like the
setting of a Hallmark movie. The title of this movie –
Welcome Home! I know it doesn't sound overly creative or
appropriate. Our child was not home at this time, but as we
prepared, it had meaning.

In Jesus' day, children were not held to be overly important
in the social pecking order. This verse from the Gospel of
Mark is a reminder to us, that the way we welcome, treat
and value children reveals a great deal about our heart.
Children had little importance at the time of Christ and the
disciples figured that forging a relationship with them was
not going to help them get ahead when it came to God's
work...or so they thought. Jesus told the disciples that to
lead they must be willing to serve the lowly, weak, and
powerless – that would include children. They must be
willing to put them first. Children were significant to the
Father.

Flashback with me once again to Christmas Eve – 1996 – to
the set of our Hallmark movie entitled *Welcome Home*.
Christmas filled the room. Beautiful stockings hung from the
fireplace as it crackled and warmed the heart. The scent of
freshly baked cookies filled the air. The twinkling lights on
the tree kept time with the holiday tunes that stirred a

barrage of Christmas memories…STOP!

To be honest, I was amazed that the holiday instrumentals were still playing in the background. At some point, those tunes usually got replaced with some action-packed movie, along with my husband's convincing argument on the importance of being "fashionably late" to the family get together. But instead of an action-packed movie, I found him writing. He seemed incredibly focused and intentional. I hated to interrupt, but couldn't help but wonder what he was doing, so I asked. He looked up from his bible and the tears welled up in his eyes. The emotions took over every ounce of restraint and those same tears that resisted in every way, now flowed down his strong cheekbones.

He expressed how much he was looking forward to having another child and how much he loved her already. He was writing her a letter to let her know she was loved and welcomed. It's amazing how much love you can hold in your heart for a child you've never met. Adopted children are absolutely born in the hearts of their parents. My husband understood what Jesus meant about welcoming the children. Those that are lowly, weak and powerless. He was willing to put her first. Jesus also instructed all who wanted to be His disciple to not only welcome the children but to be like little children - humble, meek, and without pride. These are powerful responses to what's in your heart and I am so grateful for my husband – a disciple of Christ.

The *welcome* for our adopted child began in our hearts that Christmas Eve night.

Baby Steps of Faith Personal Reflection

Mark 9:37: Whoever welcomes one of these
little children in my name welcomes me...

Baby Step 23 – How is your heart preparing to welcome a child?

Share your Story:

_____
_____
_____
_____

Trial or triumph? _____

Explain:

_____
_____
_____
_____

Personal Action Steps to Grow:

_____
_____
_____
_____

Supplication:

_____
_____
_____
_____

Lamentations 3:22-23 Because of the LORD'S great love
we are not consumed, for his compassions never fail.
They are new every morning; great is your faithfulness.

Time marches on for families of adoption, but never fast
enough. The holidays were behind us and the new year was
ahead. (1997) The wait for a child to be matched to our
family continued. It was challenging. The caseworker
graciously gave us tentative timelines, but warned us that
nothing was certain. She suggested time spent on learning
more about the Filipino culture and planning our travel
itinerary. It was going to be at least a year before we
traveled, but we welcomed any suggestion that helped us
stay busy. Most nights I found myself wrestling with God. I
continued to ask, "Why me?" I still grumbled, "This is
taking forever." Eventually, I relinquished my will for His.
The wrestling would seize and peace would find its way to
my heart. As I fell asleep in His arms, I whispered to the
Lord, "I know you still love me…I know you still care."
Lamentations tells us that *because of the Lord's great love
we are not consumed… and His compassion never fails.*

Morning arrived. Seeing the mounds of tissues, caused me to
remember my tears in the night; but I made it through.
Today was a new day. I was not consumed by despair. I was
grateful for God's love, compassion, and faithfulness that
swept over me in the night and allowed me to sleep
peacefully. I made some breakfast and pulled out my
devotional. It dared to ask this question: Are there any
children in our world who need help with some basic

necessities…a coat, a meal, a ride home? It went on to pose this thought: We might be tempted to say the problem is too big…that we can't help everyone, but that misses the point. Jesus placed great value on the life of a child.

My tears in the night and the heavy discouragement lifted as I read the devotional excerpt. I sensed God saying we were on the right road and because of His great love, it would not consume me. I was reassured that God would sustain me. There are children in the world who need us to be strong. God is full of compassion. God is faithful. Time does march on in the adoption process. Read God's Word while you wait and be encouraged in His promises to help you endure it. Keep marching on.

Baby Steps of Faith Personal Reflection

Lamentations 3:22-23 Because of the LORD'S great love
we are not consumed, for his compassions never fail.
They are new every morning; great is your faithfulness.

Baby Step 24 – Are you consumed by the waiting?

Share your Story:

_____
_____
_____
_____

Trial or triumph? _____

Explain:

_____
_____
_____
_____

Personal Action Steps to Grow:

_____
_____
_____
_____

Supplication:

_____
_____
_____
_____

Jeremiah 1:5 Before I formed you in the womb I knew
you, before you were born I set you apart...

God intimately knows each one of us before we are formed
in our mother's womb and He has set us apart for His plan
and purpose. I don't know about you, but just knowing that
we have history even before we're born, gives me
overwhelming confidence in this all-knowing, powerful God
I serve and His timing to bring a child into my life. He is the
divine creator.

**Jeremiah 1:5 "Before I formed you in the womb I knew
you, before you were born I set you apart..."** Before
Jeremiah's conception, God had a plan for him. This verse
shows how far ahead God was planning for Jeremiah. It's
the same for each of us and our adopted child.

Adopting parents conceive a child. Unlike natural parents,
they conceive according to this definition: To conceive
means to form in the mind, to think up, or have an idea, a
feeling. Natural parents define conception as the act of
getting pregnant. You may not share sexual intimacy in
order to conceive an adopted child....and announce to
family and friends that you're expecting...let's face it, the
adoption process is not the greatest aphrodisiac, but
adopting parents do conceptualize the idea of a child
through adoption and take the necessary steps to prepare for
the child's birth and arrival to their forever home.
Sometimes they conceive a child long before that child takes
residency in the mother's womb.

My husband wrote a letter to our adopted child Christmas 1996. She was born sixteen months later on April 15, 1998. She had not been conceived in the natural, but this father had conceived his daughter in his heart and mind. She had not been born when this letter was written, but he spoke to her like he knew her intimately. I want to encourage you to write a personal letter to your child and let conception take place in your heart. Let the timing of your child's birth and God's great plan for their life in the Creator's hands.

Christmas Eve 1996

Merry Christmas!

As I am sitting here, my heart longs for you to be with us as we celebrate Christmas. Even though you're not here with us today, a tear comes to my eye as I wonder what you're doing on this Christmas Day. How are you celebrating the birth of Jesus? Is someone there to love and to hold you? To give you the love every child deserves to have, not only on Christmas, but every day of the year. Do you feel a sense of belonging to your natural parents or are you wondering what's ahead of you as you wait to be adopted? Know one thing…you already have my heart. It hurts me to know you are somewhere else besides here with your forever family. My prayer today is that Jesus is loving you through someone who has a heart for children like your soon to be parents and that this process of adoption will speed up and you will come home to us where you truly belong. You are in our hearts and hopefully we are in yours.

Merry Christmas my child.

Love,

Daddy

Baby Steps of Faith Personal Reflection

Jeremiah 1:5 Before I formed you in the womb I knew you, before you were born I set you apart...

Baby Step 25 – Have you conceived yet?

Share your Story:

_____

_____

_____

_____

Trial or triumph? _____

Explain:

_____

_____

_____

_____

Personal Action Steps to Grow:

_____

_____

_____

_____

Supplication:

_____

_____

_____

_____

Isaiah 43:1 Fear not, for I have redeemed you;
I have summoned you by name,
and you are mine.

I was a teacher by occupation during our adoption adventure. I reminded my students *daily* to write their names on their papers. I reminded them *every single day*! In keeping this routine light-hearted, I often interjected a bit of humor to my request. I described to them the painstaking task their parents endured in selecting *thee perfect name*. Such as building an exhaustive list, narrowing it down to three, taking a family vote – to include extended family, and so forth. All that said, I insisted they use their perfect name!

It was time for our family to begin that very same painstaking task of naming our daughter. We knew our child was going to be a girl. Since we had a son – Kyle, it seemed only fitting for us to adopt a daughter. One day while shopping in a local department store, I came across a baby name book. Kyle and I feverishly went through the book and made a list of the names that had potential and added a few to keep the things interesting. I'll let you guess which ones kept it interesting.

Baby Names List

Kelsey   Kristin   Holly   Corrin   Chelsea   Charlotte   Dorcas

Parents take great care and put forth a lot of love in naming their child. Did you know that God calls us by *that* name? We are called the children of God (1 John 3:1) and called by name. Isn't it amazing to think that the creator of the universe, the sustainer of life, the architect of history has all the names of the redeemed inscribed in the heavens and on His hands? It is mind boggling to me that God Almighty would bother to keep each one of us in his mind from the beginning to the end of time.

The process had begun and in time we would choose a name for our precious daughter. More importantly, she would grow to love God and He would inscribe her name on His hand. Makala Myung Ok Han Kohlbrecher – our precious daughter – a child of God – called by name.

Baby Steps of Faith Personal Reflection

Isaiah 43:1 Fear not, for I have redeemed you;
I have summoned you by name,
and you are mine.

Baby Step 26 – Have you chosen thee perfect name?

Share your Story:

_____

_____

_____

_____

Trial or triumph? _____

Explain:

_____

_____

_____

_____

Personal Action Steps to Grow:

_____

_____

_____

_____

Supplication:

_____

_____

_____

_____

Hebrews 10:35-36 So do not throw away your
confidence; it will be richly rewarded. You need
to persevere so that when you have done the will
of God, you will receive what he has promised.

Cultural Training Required This was our next assignment. It
didn't take long for panic to set in when I likened culture to
refinement. I was certain we would not measure up to this
requirement – we lacked good taste! My husband, who
always sees the glass half full, was confident we would pass
this assignment. After all, we were going to be trained. What
could go wrong?

The training was not meant to refine us, but rather educate
us on a country's land, people, education, arts, customs,
religions, and ways of life. This particular training session
introduced us to the cultures of China, Korea, and the
Philippines. The workshop also provided an opportunity to
meet other adoptive parents. The day was exciting and
overwhelming at the same time. Becoming familiar with
these wonderful countries was intriguing and fascinating.
But as the training continued, I sensed my confidence
diminishing little by little. Adopted children often come
with a unique set of growing pains and complicated
questions. Allow me to share some examples:

Why was I adopted? What happened? What do you know
about my birth mother and father? Did you meet them when
I was born? Did they love me? Do you know where they are
now? What's it like in my country? Why was I placed in
America? Will I ever meet my birth parents? Is my birth day

the right day? (The exact birth dates can be difficult to determine in abandonment cases.)

These growing pains tend to surface once your child reaches the age of understanding and you begin to tell them their adoption story. These questions can arise simply because your child realizes he/she looks different from everyone else including the parents. The quest for answers to these difficult questions continues as your child grows and if left unanswered can sometimes lead to emotional challenges in your child's adult life.

I was troubled the entire trip home from cultural training. Would I be able to answer my adopted child's complicated questions? How would I handle my child's emotional challenges? I was no longer confident about adopting. I was full of fear and apprehension. One year into the process and I was ready to call it quits. I didn't sign up for a lifetime of challenges or did I? Are you losing your confidence? Don't throw it away. You need to persevere. God reassures us that we will be richly rewarded. (Hebrews 10) God chose the word *persevere* because He knew it was not going to be an easy task. If we persist in doing that which is hard and carry out the will of God, we will receive the promise - the reward. For me, that reward, that promise, was a child to a forever home. Continue to persist and trust God with your child's questions and emotional well-being. You and your child will be rewarded because you persevered.

Baby Steps of Faith Personal Reflection

Hebrews 10:35-36 So do not throw away your
confidence; it will be richly rewarded. You need
to persevere so that when you have done the will
of God, you will receive what he has promised.

Baby Step 27 – Are you confident?

Share your Story:

_____

_____

_____

_____

Trial or triumph? _____

Explain:

_____

_____

_____

_____

Personal Action Steps to Grow:

_____

_____

_____

_____

Supplication:

_____

_____

_____

_____

1 Corinthians 13:13 And now these three remain:
faith, hope and love. But the greatest of these is love.

Adoption is a process. Whether it's a meeting with a
caseworker or a cultural training weekend, you are
continually challenged to face issues that could only surface
through adoption. Our agency and conference speakers
always acknowledged God in the adoption plan – that was
the *faith* component. They presented evidence of children all
over the world in need of forever homes and we met
hundreds of adopting parents who were willing to meet that
need – that certainly demonstrated *hope*. The magnitude of
God's plan in bringing together a specific child and their
adoptive parents was continually voiced within the adoption
agency – making us all the more aware of God's great *love*
for us and his attention to details. Faith, hope and love are
all components of the adoption process. But would I have
enough of the greatest of these – love?

I know how to love a child. As a birth mother, I was
completely aware of the love I had for our son Kyle; but, I
began to question my ability to love our adopted daughter
the same way, because I hadn't given birth to her. Adoption
is a completely different process. You don't carry the child
naturally. There is no pregnancy. Once I learned I was
pregnant, to the day Kyle was born, each new experience
caused my love to grow deeper. I was keenly aware this love
for my child had developed significantly through the
pregnancy experience. I watched this precious life grow
daily within me. I gently caressed and prayed over my

womb…sang and spoke to my child. My heart was deeply in love. In the words of a great poet, I asked, "How do I love thee?" - my adopted child.

I want to encourage you to start thinking about *your* answer to that same question, "How do I love thee?" Give life to your adopted child, long before they arrive, through new and creative experiences. Start with your announcement. Design something incredibly unique and share it with family and friends. There are some great photo ideas on Pinterest and Instagram that beautifully express the heart of adoption and will cause that love to stir inside of you. Consider writing a blog or creating a Facebook page sharing highlights of your journey and updates – these will not only help you, but friends, and family will begin to connect emotionally with your child – who is not here physically. Journal your thoughts and write sweet letters to your child. Include serious thoughts and playful ones. These will serve as a wonderful keepsake. Pray continuously for your child and you will see your affection grow.

I can tell you from experience, you will discover a love you never knew you had for your adopted child and it will be overflowing. Your child is part of God's plan– have *faith*. Create new experiences as you wait for your child to arrive and fall in love – have *hope.* Your love will grow. It will be unconditional, strong and never waiver. In spite of not having them naturally, your love will come naturally - *love never fails.*

Baby Steps of Faith Personal Reflection

1 Corinthians 13:13 And now these three remain:
faith, hope and love. But the greatest of these is love.

Baby Step 28 – How do I love thee?

Share your Story:

_____
_____
_____
_____

Trial or triumph? _____

Explain:

_____
_____
_____
_____

Personal Action Steps to Grow:

_____
_____
_____
_____

Supplication:

_____
_____
_____
_____

Ephesians 2:14 For he himself is our peace, who has
made the two one and has destroyed the barrier, the
dividing wall of hostility.

A rainbow is a symbol of God's covenant with His people. It
serves as a reminder that God is faithful to keep His
promises. Rainbows appeared to us many times during the
adoption process and reminded us of God's faithfulness. The
most poignant time was when we received our homestudy
review in the midst of a storm. Another encounter took place
while attending a Filipino Festival. With excitement and
anticipation, our entire family traveled to Bensenville,
Illinois for an adoption event that was meant to give us a
deeper appreciation and understanding of the Filipino
culture – the birthplace of our adopted daughter. Kyle was
very excited about joining us for the weekend and learning
more about the Philippines.

At the hotel, we inquired about a good place to eat breakfast.
A gentleman in the lobby suggested a local eatery called
"The Rainbow Restaurant." That's ironic. To anyone else, it
was just a restaurant name, but not to this rainbow believing
family. It was no longer about a stack of pancakes – it was a
date with destiny – and only a few blocks away! Walking
down the street, Kyle spotted the diner and we dashed for
the entrance. As the waitress showed us to our table, we
realized there were not too many English speaking guests.
The rainbow restaurant lived up to its name.

There were people of every color, creed, and ethnic
background from wall to wall. Ephesians describes the Jews

and Gentiles made as one through Christ. Our family witnessed that in this place. There was conversation, laughter, and the breaking of bread together. No barriers appeared evident, no dividing walls of hostility, instead we found people enjoying people, made as one. It was a rich moment – that pot of gold at the end of the rainbow. It's powerful when we recognize the riches we gain in embracing our differences. When we destroy the dividing walls and strive for unity and two become one. It can be a rewarding experience.

Our family traveled to Bensenville for a weekend of training and returned home inspired to be one with all mankind, which lead to miles and miles of singing one simple song: Jesus loves the little children, all the children of the world. Red and yellow, black and white, they are precious in His sight – Jesus loves the little children of the world.

Baby Steps of Faith Personal Reflection

Ephesians 2:14 For he himself is our peace, who has made the two one and has destroyed the barrier, the dividing wall of hostility.

Baby Step 29 – Are you struggling with dividing walls?

Share your Story:

_____
_____
_____
_____

Trial or triumph? _____

Explain:

_____
_____
_____
_____

Personal Action Steps to Grow:

_____
_____
_____
_____

Supplication:

_____
_____
_____
_____

Hebrews 12:1 …let us throw off everything that hinders
and the sin that so easily entangles, and let us run with
perseverance the race marked out for us.

In this scripture, Paul was drawing the analogy between
running a race and the Christian experience. A runner
doesn't wear anything heavy when he runs because it will
hinder his progress in the race. Many times, races are won or
lost by seconds, because of this, even the weight of a shoe
makes a difference. If you want to win the race, you must
examine every detail and watch the amount of weight you
carry.

As Christians, we must recognize that there are things in our
lives that are hindering our walk with the Lord and things
that keep us entangled. It's sin. We will never be able to run
the race marked out for us as long as we are entrapped in
sin. Paul said to lay aside every weight. It was time for me to
examine the weights in my life. What was slowing me
down? What was robbing my joy? The honest soul will ask,
"Is this attitude, activity, this thing, a hindrance to my life
and spiritual maturity?" I discovered I had a long list of
weights. There were many ungodly ways in my life and I
needed to throw them off. God wanted to bring wonderful
change into my life. He wanted me to focus on and follow
the examples of Jesus – love, surrender, and obedience.
These changes would make me a better wife, mother, friend
and enable me to run the race set before me. There's more
good news. There is no extent to which sin can entangle us

that God's grace does not abound still more to free us. (Romans 5:20)

Are there any spiritual weights in your life? Is there anything hindering your walk with God? Anything slowing you down in the adoption race that needs to be thrown off? If so, I want to encourage you to lay them aside – take off those heavy weights. Surrender those things to the Lord and allow Him to bring change into your life. Ask Him to help you. You'll experience greater freedom and joy.

Baby Steps of Faith Personal Reflection

Hebrews 12:1 …let us throw off everything that hinders and the sin that so easily entangles, and let us run with perseverance the race marked out for us.

Baby Step 30 – What things are slowing you down?

Share your Story:

_____

_____

_____

_____

Trial or triumph? _____

Explain:

_____

_____

_____

_____

Personal Action Steps to Grow:

_____

_____

_____

_____

Supplication:

_____

_____

_____

_____

Ecclesiastes 4:12 Though one may be overpowered, two
can defend themselves. A cord of three strands is
not quickly broken.

One day I received a phone call from a friend about another
adoption opportunity in Washington D.C. A reputable
agency was seeking families willing to adopt children from
Russia. In most cases, placement happened immediately
upon approval. Was God redirecting our steps? Was he
closing the door to the Philippines and opening another
door? I spent the afternoon online gathering more
information about this Russian adoption option. I was
overpowered by this opened door and overwhelmed at the
possibility of a child being placed within six months. When
my husband got home from work, I anxiously shared
everything my friend had told me and what I had learned
online. I tried hard to keep my emotions at bay and focus on
relaying the information…sticking with the details, my heart
was leaping at this new opportunity. For me, this
conversation was simply a means of getting my husband up
to speed on this exciting new direction from the Lord. I was
certain he would be equally as excited and ready to catch the
next flight to Washington; but, he wasn't. He suggested we
pray about it and take some time to process. He said, "Just
because it's quick, doesn't mean it's the best way to go."

It didn't take long for every emotion in my body to override
the calm and informative approach that began the
conversation and I replied with an explosion of emotion,
"What on earth is there to think about? We could be

traveling in a few months to get our baby!" Needless to say, my husband learned to avoid these three words – *take our time* – in all future conversations regarding the adoption. I was hurt and confused. Our marriage and faith were being tried. Weeks went by and very little speaking took place. My husband was uncertain about the opportunity in Washington D.C. He believed we needed to stay on our present course. I could hardly bare it.

Desiring to have children and struggling with infertility can strain a marriage. Being single and convincing friends and family that adoption will fill your desires to parent, can bring strife when they don't agree. Adoption overall can bring different challenges to relationships. *A cord of three strands is not easily broken* can pertain to any relationship. As fate would have it, this was the verse on our wedding invitation. When two people are being pulled, to the point of tearing, by hardships or strife, the temptation to part may seem like the only option. But there is always hope, when we allow the divine third strand into the equation. Our unity is not easily broken, when we invite God to be more than a bystander in our marriages, families, and friendships. When two hearts are open to the Spirit and we humbly take our conflicts and weaknesses to God, love conquers. Extend grace and forgiveness…learn to walk in love in times of conflict.

Baby Steps of Faith Personal Reflection

Ecclesiastes 4:12 Though one may be overpowered, two
can defend themselves. A cord of three strands is
not quickly broken.

Baby Step 31 – Who is pulling your cord?

Share your Story:

_____

_____

_____

_____

Trial or triumph? _____

Explain:

_____

_____

_____

_____

Personal Action Steps to Grow:

_____

_____

_____

_____

Supplication:

_____

_____

_____

_____

Psalm 40:8 I desire to do your will, O my God;
your law is within my heart.

What's your opinion? I could not stop thinking about the
Russian adoption opportunity. I was hoping to somehow
persuade my husband that it was all part of a new plan – a
new direction. In the meantime, I decided to pursue the
counsel of others to help build my persuasive case. This is
not all that unusual for the human condition. We often seek
advice or the support of others when we have a big decision
to make. We look to a trusted friend, co-worker, a neighbor,
family member or clergy. Some of us look to God; but, most
of us decide without looking to God for direction. We make
a decision which seems best to us, get a multitude of others
to agree, reinforce our position, and run with it.

I recall one conversation in my crusade for support that
didn't quite go the way I had anticipated. I was telling a
friend from church about the latest opportunity to adopt
from Russia, the need for families, and immediate
placement. I explained that our current agency had no
definite baby arrival time and we were in this dreadful
waiting game. I shared how my son's rainbow posters
adorned the fireplace just the night before the phone call in
my attempt to help her visualize the timing and almost
providential hand of God in this opportunity. I had
prepared my defense extremely well. Maybe the poster
visual was a stretch. I was certain my friend would agree
without question, but instead, she gave godly counsel. How
do I know that? Godly counsel speaks biblical truth in love.

She reminded me that God does not communicate through "signs" alone, but in prayer and in the reading of His Word. She simply asked if I had prayed about the decision to pursue the Russian adoption. She asked me if I had spent any time in God's Word?

Circumstances, signs and wonders, happen every day in our lives, but we can't rely on them alone to know the will of God. My friend recalled the events that lead us to our current agency a year ago and how God established that decision in His word. She encouraged me to revisit my journal notes and spend some time in prayer. I took her advice and looked over the beginning days of my adoption journal – penned over a year ago. I took it a step further and reviewed and read everything I could on knowing God's will and seeking His direction. Hearing His voice was important, especially since I had come to a fork in the road – which my husband didn't see at all.

Four areas to consider when seeking God's direction:

1. Read the Word of God with regard to your decision
2. Pray and meditate on the scriptures that God gives to you in your quiet time
3. Journal experiences that take place
4. Seek Godly counsel – a Pastor or a long time follower of Christ

Are you seeking God's direction in your adoption? Do you truly desire to do God's will as the psalmist declared? Go after God's opinion with all your heart and exercise these four steps regularly. You'll find God and the direction He has for you.

Baby Steps of Faith Personal Reflection

Psalm 40:8 I desire to do your will, O my God;
your law is within my heart.

Baby Step 32 – In seeking God, which of the four areas requires more practice?

Share your Story:

_____

_____

_____

_____

Trial or triumph? _____

Explain:

_____

_____

_____

_____

Personal Action Steps to Grow:

_____

_____

_____

_____

Supplication:

_____

_____

_____

_____

Ephesians 4:2-3 Be completely humble and gentle; be
patient, bearing with one another in love. Make
every effort to keep the unity of the Spirit
through the bond of peace.

The agency in Washington D.C. continued to place children
in adopting homes. I would occasionally revisit the option
with my husband to see if he had reconsidered. I diligently
tried to create a balance between seeking God and soliciting
the advice of others as to our role, if any, in contacting this
agency. This is incredibly hard for a woman. We have this
insatiable desire to talk and know what others think.
Inquiring minds want to know! Thank God for His Spirit
that not only leads us, but watches over us, and extends
mercy when we are determined to get our way.

All that said, I found a new friend to talk to and I told her
every detail regarding the Russian adoption option. I loved
the fact that she was such a good listener. She let me go on
endlessly and waited patiently for an opportunity to share
her thoughts. I remember the tenderness behind her counsel
as she spoke. Rather than dismiss the possibility of this being
a new direction from the Lord, she challenged me to
consider a couple of key points in my search for
confirmation. She, too, continued to speak the truth in love
(biblical point stated gently), "It is very important that you
and your husband are in *agreement* and the fact that you are
not, may be all God will use to reveal that the Russian door
is not His will." The Holy Spirit began to speak to my heart
about agreement and unity.

While it's not always easy to get a couple or group of people to agree on something, it usually can be done. After all, agreements are mutually beneficial. You may not get everything you want, but you'll most likely get closer than you would have on your own. It's important to be in agreement. It makes life easier. But Ephesians speaks about unity and that's more important than agreement. Webster defines unity as "the quality or state of not being multiple – oneness." For oneness to be achieved your vision for everything would have to align.

I thought about the words of my friend and the meaning of unity. It was conclusive, Kurt and I were not in agreement, nor was there unity. There was no longer oneness in our adoption vision – no alignment. I want to warn you about disagreements in your adoption pursuit and the importance of unity. Disagreement can open the door for Satan to come in and bring confusion, pride, and disharmony. I let those practices enter my marriage. It was time to examine my motives and live out the true meaning of Christian unity – put others first. That moment, I realized the importance of keeping unity in my marriage – to be completely humble, gentle, patient, and bear with one another in love. If I truly wanted to hear from God and receive direction on this decision, I had to begin living these important steps – starting with my husband. Guard the unity in your relationships and make every effort to walk in peace.

Baby Steps of Faith Personal Reflection

Ephesians 4:2-3 Be completely humble and gentle; be
patient, bearing with one another in love. Make
every effort to keep the unity of the Spirit
through the bond of peace.

Baby Step 33 – Any relationship(s) struggling to maintain unity?

Share your Story:

_____

_____

_____

_____

Trial or triumph? _____

Explain:

_____

_____

_____

_____

Personal Action Steps to Grow:

_____

_____

_____

_____

Supplication:

_____

_____

_____

_____

Matthew 18:21-22 Peter asked, "LORD, how many times
shall I forgive...Jesus answered, "I tell you, not seven
times, but seventy-seven times."

It can be difficult to have conversations with acquaintances,
friends, and even family when you're in the adoption
process. They mean well, but sometimes forget the roads
we've traveled like –Singles Street, Infertility Lane,
Miscarriage Turnpike, and Hysterectomy Highway – for
starters. Many of you have traveled these roads and now
you're on the Adoption Freeway; but, it has not lived up to
its name! If anything, it's added a few new twists and turns
to the journey. Everyone's got an opinion on the Adoption
Freeway! You have been crushed by life's unbearable sorrow
and trouble. That said, we long for the compassionate heart
of people, but our paths often cross with the critical heart of
people. Before you know it, bitterness, resentment, and
unforgiveness find their way to your heart.

Matthew 18:22 tells us to forgive not seven times, but
seventy-seven times. King James states 70 x 7, but that does
not mean you only have to forgive 490 times. You must
forgive for a life time. Harboring unforgiveness will ruin
your health. It's poison to your body. It took some time for
me to realize that unforgiveness was hurting me more than
the person who had wronged me. I always thought it
seemed unfair for that individual to receive forgiveness
when I was hurting. I got hurt and they got freedom without
paying for the pain they had caused. Now I realize that I'm
helping myself when I choose to forgive. It releases God to

do His work in me and my faith is built stronger; whereas, unforgiveness hinders our faith from working. I'm happier and feel better physically when I forgive others.

Keep Satan from outwitting you (2 Corinthians 2:10-11) and convincing you to hold onto your hurt and anger. Don't assist him in the torment. Be quick to forgive. Pray for those who hurt you. They may not even be aware of it, or maybe they are so self-centered they don't care. Either way, they need a revelation from the Lord. You have too much at stake. Your fellowship with Jesus, your health, and fulfilling the call God has on your life to be a parent of adoption. Keep your heart in the right place and enjoy the Adoption Freeway.

Baby Steps of Faith Personal Reflection

Matthew 18:21-22 Peter asked, "LORD, how many times shall I forgive…Jesus answered, "I tell you, not seven times, but seventy-seven times."

Baby Step 34 – Harboring any unforgiveness?

Share your Story:

_____
_____
_____
_____

Trial or triumph? _____

Explain:

_____
_____
_____
_____

Personal Action Steps to Grow:

_____
_____
_____
_____

Supplication:

_____
_____
_____
_____

Matthew 18:19-20 Again, I tell you that if two of you
on earth agree about anything you ask for, it will be
done for you by my Father in heaven. For where two or
three come together in my name, there am I with them.

Examining your heart and taking responsibility for your
actions can be liberating. I spent regular time with the Lord,
reading the Word, and praying. It brought peace and
contentment back into my life and a renewed strength in the
adoption wait. Summer was coming to a close and my
thoughts had turned from the Russian adoption paperwork,
which was still sitting on my desk waiting on my husband's
approval, to writing classroom curriculum notes, creating
bulletin boards, and developing class projects in preparation
for the new school year.

I had finished working in my classroom one day and headed
for home. I found myself lost in my thoughts, as I drove
aimlessly along the country roads. I began to reflect on the
last few months of the adoption journey. The Holy Spirit
called to remembrance the wise counsel of friends and the
scriptures that He had been speaking to my heart during my
daily quiet time. For the first time in months, everything was
clear in my mind. I had resolved to be still, to talk less, and
listen more, and then I heard His voice in the stillness of a
drive in the country. He told me to maintain my position at
Lifelink Adoption Agency. I didn't hear God audibly speak,
but once again, He spoke to my heart and directed me to
maintain my position. Tears rolled down my face as I
realized this meant more waiting, but God assured me that

He would give me the strength and I was not waiting in vain. He had only the best for me.

Only God can change a heart, heal the sick, restore a marriage, and more. We can wear ourselves out trying to accomplish something, but when we finally surrender our will for the Father's, we make progress. I knew it was God because I was content with His answer – full of peace. The burden of decision was lifted. I found rest. I couldn't wait to tell my husband about this God-defining moment, ask forgiveness, and thank him for leading our family strong and diligently.

Pray for God's direction in choosing an adoption agency. Agree together and seal it with a hearty Amen! – which means "so be it." Don't waiver in your decision – that only brings doubt and confusion. Line up your speech and actions with your decision. "So be it" means the matter is closed. A door to sin is open when we don't submit our plans to God's will and suddenly speak contrary to what God is doing and what was agreed upon. Guard against selfish ambition. It will bring strife and confusion into your household and in your relationships.

Are you wavering in your adoption decision? Take it to God, tell Him your sorry for doubting, reinforce your original decree, and move forward. Don't be discouraged. Remember there's great power in agreement. God promises where two or more are gathered, there He is, and anything they ask for in His will, it shall be done.

Baby Steps of Faith Personal Reflection

Matthew 18:19-20 Again, I tell you that if two of you
on earth agree about anything you ask for, it will be
done for you by my Father in heaven. For where two or
three come together in my name, there am I with them.

Baby Step 35 – Any wavering in your adoption decision?

Share your Story:

_____
_____
_____
_____

Trial or triumph? _____

Explain:

_____
_____
_____
_____

Personal Action Steps to Grow:

_____
_____
_____
_____

Supplication:

_____
_____
_____
_____

Ecclesiastes 3:1 There is a time for everything, and
a season for every activity under heaven.

There is a season for *every activity* under heaven. In
adoption, the goal is to *stay busy* in every season as you
wait for your child to arrive. It would be nice to know when.
Unfortunately, in adoption, those specifics are not part of the
package. Some agencies give you a tentative arrival date, but
delays are probable. Expecting parents go to the doctor, get a
confirmed pregnancy, and a wonderful due date. It's not
exact science, but one's natural delivery generally runs close
to that given due date. If not, they have cause to worry.

In adoption, the baby's due date is called the arrival date.
You only move as fast as the paperwork, clearances,
collecting finances, travel arrangements, and last, but not
least, the meeting of all international and state requirements,
which vary greatly from country to country. It can take
months figuring it all out and several more months to
complete the process. It's a daunting task as you apply and
complete time-sensitive documents only to have them expire
within a year and repeat the process. Today adopting
parents also have heightened security issues due to terrorists
attacks and child sex-trafficking, both of which can cause
extra screening and delays.

You will make futile attempts to try and figure out a possible
arrival date. Through ongoing communication with your
caseworker, you will chart timelines and run comparisons
with other adoptive parents within the agency, and try to
project a date. Of course, one always hopes a child will be

placed surprisingly quick and they beat the odds of a long wait. Our adoption process was in its nineteenth month and still no news of a child or an arrival date. It was evident that God's ways and timing of our child's arrival was not ours to determine.

Your adoption from start to finish could take months or years. Sadly, your child's arrival date is as predictable as the weather. Keep your sense of humor. There is a season for every activity under heaven and this is your season to complete any and all adoption *activities* – prepare your child's room and keep your personal calendar full. Stay engaged in the process and bring your child home! There is a time for everything and God knows the specific arrival date. In the meantime, He called you and is faithful to equip you. The goal is to stay busy in this waiting season, even if it means repeating expired steps. A child's life depends on you. I repeat, keep busy!

Baby Steps of Faith Personal Reflection

Ecclesiastes 3:1 There is a time for everything, and
a season for every activity under heaven.

Baby Step 36 – How are you staying busy?

Share your Story:

_____

_____

_____

_____

Trial or triumph? _____

Explain:

_____

_____

_____

_____

Personal Action Steps to Grow:

_____

_____

_____

_____

Supplication:

_____

_____

_____

_____

Philippians 4:11,13 I am not saying this because I am in
need, for I have learned to be content whatever the
circumstances. I can do everything through him
who gives me strength.

Webster defines contentment as satisfied; being pleased;
happiness. How I long to be in that place where I walk
content in all circumstances of my life. However, at this
point in the adoption process and life in general, I *am
learning* to be content in any and every situation. With
another school year behind me, I am looking forward to
summer days. We continue to wait for a referral – the
paperwork of an available child – from the beautiful Filipino
country.

Some friends of ours invited us to join their family for a
summer retreat at a Y.M.C.A. camp in southern Missouri. A
few days communing with nature did sound relaxing.
However, the kids had other plans like swimming, funyaks,
and volleyball. I thought we came to relax? Little did we
realize that this weekend would bring both physical and
spiritual breakthroughs.

One evening both families decided to take a long walk to
burn off some dinner calories. We hiked a few woodland
trails, but eventually made our way back to the main roads.
Honestly, the mission was more about finding the
campground ice-cream shop than calorie burning. Our noses
led us right to the sugar cones. The Dad's took the children
and our ice-cream order, while my friend Kelly and I found
a picnic table nearby and sat to chat.

My sweet friend seemed pre-occupied in her thoughts during the hike. She was quiet and the conversation was reserved. But as our families made a dash to the ice-cream shop, we were left to ourselves and the conversation went from zero to sixty. Maybe we just needed our own space. Wasting little time, she leaned over and shared some exciting news. She was pregnant! In the wake of her announcement, she was so sensitive to my emotions and handled both the news and me with such care. Her husband was inside the ice-cream shop sharing the news with their children and my husband, while she chose to share privately in case it was difficult for me.

Baby announcements from friends and family can be emotionally challenging in the uncertainty and wait of your child. But as Paul writes, we have to learn to be content in our circumstances.

I rejoiced that evening for many reasons. I celebrated Kelly's wonderful news of a new baby in the spring. I was also thankful for this precious woman who understood the difficulty of the adoption wait and because of her concern, chose to share her news privately. This is an example of a dear friend. I was grateful to the Lord, because like Paul, I realized that I was indeed learning to be content in my circumstances. I was satisfied, pleased, and happy because of God's strength in me and the certainty of His great love for me and my child.

Baby Steps of Faith Personal Reflection

Philippians 4:11,13 I am not saying this because I am in
need, for I have learned to be content whatever the
circumstances. I can do everything through him
who gives me strength.

Baby Step 37 – Are you learning to be content in whatever the circumstances?

Share your Story:

_____
_____
_____
_____

Trial or triumph? _____

Explain:

_____
_____
_____
_____

Personal Action Steps to Grow:

_____
_____
_____
_____

Supplication:

_____
_____
_____
_____

Numbers 12:6 Listen to my words…I reveal myself
to him in visions, I speak to him in dreams.

God's Word is full of stories where He supernaturally
revealed Himself to His people. In the Old Testament the
people would mark these God encounters with a stone. The
stone was a memorial for future generations and a reminder
of God's faithfulness and power. God worked miraculously
through my expectant friend Kelly and this extraordinary
happening would change our lives forever. In the wake of
her announcement, I assured her that God was doing a work
in my heart and each baby announcement was another
opportunity for me to be content with my circumstances and
to trust God to deliver my child in His perfect time. I had
come to a place of surrender and rest in His provision. I
celebrated her good news. Having a child is a wonderful
miracle and in order for God to continue to bless my life, I
had to celebrate the blessings of others

Numbers 12:6 tells us that God reveals Himself in visions
and dreams. God was about to do something neither of us
had ever experienced before. Troubled about how to share
her pregnancy news, my friend prayed for wisdom. One
night, God gave Kelly a dream and spoke these words,
**"When the news of your baby's arrival is shared with
others, your friend's child will also be born."** Can you
believe it? How amazing is this great God we serve? My
heart leaped for joy when Kelly shared this incredible
moment with me. I had a due date! If nothing else, I had a
season – spring – our child would be born in the spring!

Our time line was no longer illusive. This was unbelievable. It was too good to be true. It was a miraculous encounter with the Living God. I may not have physically marked it with an Old Testament stone; but I will never forget God's great love for me and His faithfulness in bringing me this good news.

A few weeks later my God-seeking friend went to see her doctor and called to confirm my approximate due date. With great confidence in the Lord, she declared - **March 23, 1998.** It came to pass, and they gave birth to their son on that very day. According to the Words God gave her, it was safe to say that our daughter would be born at or around March 23, 1998. In all likelihood her referral would be available a few short months thereafter. This filled us with such anticipation and expectation in the remainder of our wait. Our daughter's referral paperwork came in July, 1998. A beautiful photo and her birth information was included. She was born **April 15, 1998** – just three weeks after the birth of Kelly's son. God is so amazing and faithful.

Baby Steps of Faith Personal Reflection

Numbers 12:6 Listen to my words...I reveal myself
to him in visions, I speak to him in dreams.

Baby Step 38 – Any miracles to shout about?

Share your Story:

_____
_____
_____
_____

Trial or triumph? _____

Explain:

_____
_____
_____
_____

Personal Action Steps to Grow:

_____
_____
_____
_____

Supplication:

_____
_____
_____
_____

> 2 Chronicles 32:7-8 Be strong and courageous. Do not
> be afraid or discouraged...for there is a greater
> power with us than with them...with us is the
> LORD our God to help us and to fight our battles.

Strong and courageous are two words that best describe a
parent of adoption. You will experience days of fear,
discouragement, and battle fatigue. Some days your
confidence will waiver on this mission. You'll second guess
your decision to enlist and question your effectiveness in
this battle. You may be tempted, on more than one occasion,
to wave a white flag and surrender. You have signed up to
deliver the orphans from captivity but find yourself
confronted with battle after battle. You have a real enemy.
Satan is your adversary. He is the father of all darkness and
children living in institutions, orphanages, parentless,
homeless, and poverty-stricken are all part of that darkness.
It's not God's best or plan, so we wage war, sign on to rescue
them, and keep at it until we triumphantly bring them home
for good.

Powerful, militant emotions fill me up today. Seems strange,
given the fact that I am coordinating a charitable holiday
drive. Perhaps you're familiar with "Operation Christmas
Child." As Peer Advisor of my school, I thought it would be
a great giving project for the student body. Here's how it
works. Students fill shoeboxes with Christmas toys, candy,
hygiene items, etc... and deliver them to the nearest nation-
wide drop site. From there, boxes are loaded onto cargo
planes and delivered to children all over the world. Many of

these children live in poverty, orphanages, and war-torn countries. Receiving these shoeboxes will be the highlight of the holiday season and minister to families in need. As I loaded hundreds of shoeboxes in the car and drove to the nearest drop-site, I began to think about the acquiring children. Many of them are orphans who need loving parents and a home. It didn't make sense to me. For eighteen months we have battled to provide these very things – love and provision to a child in need – yet, we're still waiting for a child. Why does it have to be so complicated and time consuming? It's seems simple enough. There's a child in need and a family ready to meet that need…done. Yet, we battle for months, some years, before we triumphantly bring home a child in need.

Remember when Jesus over-turned the market tables in the temple because it wasn't right? I am having a similar moment. Do you have some righteous anger in your heart? It can be a good thing. Learn to use it in fortifying your determination to bring children out of poverty, orphanages, and war-torn countries by battling any injustice the enemy fires your way. The injustice of bureaucracy, endless paperwork, clearances, delays, absorbent fees, and endless waiting. Stay determined – keep standing – fighting – praying – and bring a child out of these conditions. Thank God for adoption advocates, agencies, and people with a heart to adopt, because at the end of the day, all of us are willing to stay in the battle until every child has a forever home. Your child is so blessed to have you fighting the good fight. They will witness first-hand the heart of God through your love, compassion, and desire to give them a life full of hope and purpose. All of this makes your enemy fight harder against you but *be strong and courageous for there is a greater power with you than with your enemy.* The Lord will help you in the battle. Prepare to come out victorious.

Baby Steps of Faith Personal Reflection

2 Chronicles 32:7-8 Be strong and courageous. Do not be afraid or discouraged...for there is a greater power with us than with them...with us is the LORD our God to help us and to fight our battles.

Baby Step 39 – What's your biggest battle?

Share your Story:

_____
_____
_____
_____

Trial or triumph? _____

Explain:

_____
_____
_____
_____

Personal Action Steps to Grow:

_____
_____
_____
_____

Supplication:

_____
_____
_____
_____

Psalm 37:4 Delight yourself in the LORD, and
He will give you the desires of your heart.

I love to linger in the presence of the Lord. More often, I like
to *hide* myself in His presence. Hide away from the noise
and troubles of life – seeking His refuge. I sometimes get a
mental picture of myself nestling in His wings or resting my
head on His lap like a child. It's a warm, comfortable, and a
peaceful place. I love to worship the Lord in song. I find
music takes me to that hiding place where I enjoy and rest in
the presence of God. Music ushers in an atmosphere that
helps me to speak to God – pray, hear from God – listen, and
respond to God – worship. One day, I was listening to an
instrumental song that really ministered to me. King Saul
experienced the benefits of beautiful, anointed music to
drive away his sadness each time David played his harp
(1 Samuel 16). In my case, it was a piano tune that lifted my
heaviness. I played it over and over again because with
every note I felt tremendous peace and close fellowship with
the living God. I wanted to respond to the Lord – to give
something back to Him. I began to add lyrics to the melody
and found myself creating and singing a new song to Jesus.

I loved singing that new song during quiet times, the car,
and even the shower. I was putting on a garment of praise in
place of my gloominess. Each time it rolled off my lips, it
brought me into God's presence. He would fill me with
whatever I needed that day…peace, strength, joy…God
filled me up. I was *delighting myself in the Lord.* This means
to fully yield yourself into God's hands. The more resigned

you are to God's care and keeping, the more indifferent you'll be to the conditions around you. The scripture tells us that if we delight ourselves in the Lord, He will give you the desires of your heart. When you spend time communing with God, you desire what He wants.

I believe God has given you a desire to adopt a child. Spend time in His presence so He can fill you up with peace, strength, joy…whatever you need. Keep trusting and committing your adoption to Him and in time it will come to pass. After months of enjoying my new song, curiosity took over and I decided to check out the actual title to the lovely instrumental tune that resulted in song-writing to Jesus. I chuckled as I read, "Dreams Come True."

Baby Steps of Faith Personal Reflection

Psalm 37:4 Delight yourself in the LORD, and
He will give you the desires of your heart.

Baby Step 40 – How do you usher in the presence of God?

Share your Story:

_____

_____

_____

_____

Trial or triumph? _____

Explain:

_____

_____

_____

_____

Personal Action Steps to Grow:

_____

_____

_____

_____

Supplication:

_____

_____

_____

_____

Philippians 4:6-7 Do not be anxious about anything,
but in everything, by prayer and petition, with
thanksgiving, present your requests to God.

Do not be anxious about anything. I try. It's a tall order for
the adopting parent. Today isn't all bad. I'm two for three –
praying about everything and thankful, but dealing with
some anxiety. It's another birthday for this waiting mother
and that's one step closer to having a time bomb for a
biological clock! Today, it's all about *numbers*. You'll find
yourself fretting over your birthday *number – a.k.a. age*
especially when it falls somewhere between thirty and forty
because you are very much aware that you are pushing the
limits physically. Let's face it, you don't carry and give birth
in adoption, but you still need to be physically fit to raise a
child and youthfulness has its advantages.

I find myself playing mathematician and thinking about
numbers all the time. For example, when our adopted child
turns five, our oldest child will be thirteen and I will be forty
something. At this rate, I will be raising another teenager
when I am fifty. Get the picture? Then, add in our current
584 days of waiting for a child and you can see how all these
numbers makes a woman anxious in terms of her biological
clock. How about you?

I decided to get a Godly perspective on *numbers*. I literally
took a closer look at the Book of *Numbers* in the Bible and
was surprised to see the symbolism between my adoption
journey and the journey of the Israelites. *Numbers* is a book
that describes how the Israelites came out of Egyptian

slavery and grew up in the wilderness. It has been called "The Book of Journeyings" and "The Book of Murmurings." *Numbers* records the tragic story and consequences of Israel's unbelief. What could have been an eleven day journey turned out to be a forty year ordeal! I know I have learned some things on my 584 days in the wilderness. I have been enslaved by my infertility thoughts and paralyzed by fear. Many of those days in the wilderness were spent in unbelief and full of murmurings. Just like the Israelites, I wondered if God would come through for me and if I would ever see the promise land. Can you relate?

The Book of *Numbers* also tells us about a Godly man who led the Israelites out of Egypt. His name was Moses and I believe everyone can learn from this great leader. He made mistakes on his forty year journey in the wilderness. However, in spite of his frail humanity, the significant thing about Moses is that he endured. He was steadfast. How was he able to remain steadfast? He continued to look through eyes of faith at his circumstances and believed God would deliver. Next time you become anxious looking at the *numbers* that effect your adoption journey, reflect on the Book of *Numbers* and like Moses, grow in the wilderness days and continue to be steadfast and endure. Look with eyes of faith and trust God to deliver.

Baby Steps of Faith Personal Reflection

Philippians 4:6-7 Do not be anxious about anything,
but in everything, by prayer and petition, with
thanksgiving, present your requests to God.

Baby Step 41 – Numbers got you anxious?

Share your Story:

_____
_____
_____
_____

Trial or triumph? _____

Explain:

_____
_____
_____
_____

Personal Action Steps to Grow:

_____
_____
_____
_____

Supplication:

_____
_____
_____
_____

John 16:33 I have told you these things, so that in me you
may have peace. In the world you will have trouble.
But take heart! I have overcome the world.

T'was the night before Christmas... all the stockings
were hung by the chimney with care, in hopes that
our baby soon would be there.

It's hard to believe a second Christmas has come and gone
and still no child. It's really hard. Is it God's will if *it's hard*?
I often thought that if it was hard for me, if things didn't go
smooth in my life, then it must be a sign that I am not in the
will of God and heading in the wrong direction. I have
learned over the years that the exact opposite is true. In fact,
I believe life can be the *hardest* when we are in the perfect
will of God. How will we respond to hard times?

God told us we would have troubles and trials. John 16:33
says, "I have told you these things, so that in me you may
have peace. In the world you will have trouble. But take
heart! I have overcome the world." Why would God allow
trials? Because as terrible as they are, they are good for our
spiritual development. Romans 5:3-4 says, "And not only
that, but we also glory in tribulation; knowing that
tribulation produces perseverance; and perseverance;
character; and character, hope." We are suppose to glory in
tribulation because in it we grow.

God uses these hard times to build a backbone of steel in us
and to produce character. You will need both of these things

to endure the adoption process and overall see your life's dreams and visions come to pass. I am here to tell you that whatever battles you may be fighting, no matter what obstacles lie before you, or struggles you're dealing with, there's victory in Jesus. God will give you the grace to go through trials. Life is **hard**. The adoption process is **hard**. But God said, "Be of good cheer, I have overcome the world." That my friend is the end result…we are overcomers. God enables us to conquer and defeat the **hard** stuff. He helps us to prevail in life and gain the victory. That's right…we win.

Baby Steps of Faith Personal Reflection

John 16:33 I have told you these things, so that in me you may have peace. In the world you will have trouble. But take heart! I have overcome the world.

Baby Step 42 – What's hard for you right now?

Share your Story:

_____
_____
_____
_____

Trial or triumph? _____

Explain:

_____
_____
_____
_____

Personal Action Steps to Grow:

_____
_____
_____
_____

Supplication:

_____
_____
_____
_____

> 1 Samuel 1:27 I prayed for this child, and the
> LORD has granted me what I asked of him.

Are you praying fervently for a child? Hannah prayed for a child. She went to the tabernacle to worship the Lord. She prayed and asked God to give her a son. Allow me to describe the details of Hannah's prayer time. Her lips were moving, but no sound was coming from her mouth. Hannah was praying silently. Eli, the high priest and judge, witnessed the whole thing and thought she was drunk with wine. He confronted Hannah and she assured him that she was not drunk at all, but sorrowful and pouring her heart out to God for a child. Eli understood the heart of this servant and told her to go in peace because the Lord was going to answer her prayers and give her a child. I love this story because I can relate to Hannah – a desperate woman praying for a child. But there's more to grasp in this story. Hannah was a changed person after her encounter with Eli. This barren woman was told that the Lord was going to give her a child. She believed the words of the High Priest; but, more importantly, she knew in her heart that she could depend on God. Hannah had a baby boy and named him Samuel, which means, "heard by God."

Remember Hannah and know God hears and will answer your desperate cry. Years ago, I wrote a letter with the same longing in my heart as Hannah. Like this woman, my situation of barrenness and crying out to God, changed my life in dramatic ways. God used it to move me closer to Him. Even the waiting, which was the most challenging part, taught me to trust and depend on Him. After our adoption was finalized, I noted that our daughter's birth mother was four months pregnant when I penned this letter. I would endure much more waiting beyond the moments penned in the letter that follows. However, my journal notes also reflected a changed heart over the duration of the wait. Hannah was changed dramatically from her experience in the temple, because she believed the words of the High Priest, and knew she could count on God. My own God encounters had changed my heart dramatically. I would learn to rest, to yield to the plan, and trust God's timing. Let my stories be an encouragement to you. God is using your situation to draw you closer to Him, to dramatically change you, and advance His purpose for your life. I declare the words of Eli. Go in peace because the Lord is going to answer your heart-filled prayers for a child and His timing is perfect.

Christmas Eve 1997

Dear Makala,

It has been one year since I found your Daddy writing a letter to you. We were so excited to know that our papers were in the Philippines and the matching process was underway. Your Daddy was full of emotion that morning as he thought about you. Were you born yet? If so, what were you doing? Would someone be holding you Christmas morning and singing you lullabies? We would have to continue to pray and wait on God.

Another year has passed since that tear-filled Daddy moment. Now, I find myself reflecting and writing to you this Christmas. It's a Mommy moment. We were so hoping you would be home. If nothing else, we hoped for a referral, a photo, something to hold dear to our hearts until your arrival day. I bought you a stocking for the mantle and I attached an angel pin to remind me that God is watching over you. I pray for you every day. Kyle is so anxious for you to come home. He can't wait to be a big brother. He just celebrated his 7th birthday – and blew out the candles on his cake and wished extra hard that you would come home soon. I will try not to be sad this year. I am learning to depend on God. I know He hears my prayers and answers the cries of my heart. I love you so much it amazes me!

Mommy

Baby Steps of Faith Personal Reflection

1 Samuel 1:27 I prayed for this child, and the
LORD has granted me what I asked of him.

Baby Step 43 – How have God-encounters dramatically changed you?

Share your Story:

_____
_____
_____
_____

Trial or triumph? _____

Explain:

_____
_____
_____
_____

Personal Action Steps to Grow:

_____
_____
_____
_____

Supplication:

_____
_____
_____
_____

1 Thessalonians 5:11 Therefore encourage one
another and build each other up…

This verse in 1 Thessalonians describes best what
encouragement does for another person – it builds them up.
God will bring many encouragers to you as you travel the
adoption road. One that stands out amongst the crowd was
our caseworker. Becky was the first person I met the day I
stopped by the adoption agency to pick up an information
packet. I will never forget her warm, friendly, soft-spoken
voice and smile. I immediately felt comfortable. Once we
decided to work with Lifelink, we were thrilled that Becky
was assigned as our caseworker. She completed our homestudy and knew every detail of our lives – and she still liked
us. Caseworkers definitely know all about their clients –
their strengths and weaknesses. There are *no* secrets!

Becky had a gift – to impart encouragement. There was
simply *no visible weakness* in her clients and if there was,
she handled it professionally and with a heart of
compassion. She always magnified your strengths and saw
endless potential in each client. Even the areas that needed
improvement were attainable if you were on Becky's team.

Becky was our cheerleader. She helped us to run the race.
Her continual encouragement *built us up*. She not only
displayed a servant's heart towards her perspective
adopting parent(s), but she was full of compassion for the
orphaned child. Her eyes welled up with each referral that
came across the fax machine because that meant a parentless
child would finally have a family and wonderful future.

Becky was a woman of great faith. She loved the Lord and continually reassured us that God had a plan and purpose in every adoption case.

After years of working with Becky, the agency announced her relocation and assigned us a new caseworker. Her leaving was incredibly difficult for us. I really wasn't sure how I would get to the finish line without her and naturally, I wanted her to be a part of our child's arrival. In spite of the miles between us now, I was grateful that our paths had crossed on our adoption journey. She made a big difference in our lives with her gift of encouragement.

Has God brought a "Becky" to encourage you in the adoption process? Send a card or a note and tell them what an impact they have had on your life. Becky encouraged me to journal when we started the adoption process. I hope and pray you are being renewed today as you read *Baby Steps of Faith* which was written from the notes of that original journal. May the stories, scriptures, and truth *build you up* as you travel your adoption road.

Baby Steps of Faith Personal Reflection

1 Thessalonians 5:11 Therefore encourage one
another and build each other up…

Baby Step 44 – Who is building you up with encouragement?

Share your Story:

_____
_____
_____
_____

Trial or triumph? _____

Explain:

_____
_____
_____
_____

Personal Action Steps to Grow:

_____
_____
_____
_____

Supplication:

_____
_____
_____
_____

Psalm 57:7 My heart is steadfast, O God, my heart is
steadfast; I will sing and make music.

Our agency has fellowship gatherings every few months. All
the families "in waiting" and those who are celebrating the
arrival of their children are encouraged to attend. Our family
decided to mark the calendar and catch up with others in the
adoption process. Many had received referrals and it was
picture sharing mania. Several families actually had their
newly adopted children at the gathering and it was time to
celebrate!

I'll never forget the family who had just returned home from
the Philippines with their little boy. It only took six months;
but, let me tell you, this new mommy had a steadfast heart
that had been tested, tried, and proven. The couple had
endured years of infertility obstacles and insurmountable
losses; but, because they had an unwavering heart full of
purpose, it was time to introduce their son to everyone.
Their joy was complete.

Another family had a five year old son and applied to adopt
a little girl from China. After one year in the process, China
abruptly closed its doors to American adoptions for political
reasons. They were heart-broken. They had to make a
decision and quickly because her husband was forty-four
years old and in another year he would not be an age-
appropriate applicant – a nice way of saying "too old." The
couple decided to start over and adopt from South Korea. A
referral came about a year later, right before his next
birthday, cutting it extremely close on the age restriction.

A little Korean girl would be arriving shortly. Again, with two years into the process, the steadfast heart, fixed and resolved, proudly shared with everyone a referral photo of their beautiful daughter. Their joy was complete.

Our family, now waiting about sixteen months for a referral, continued to have a steadfast heart. That's a heart that maintains a God connection in order to keep a faith vision. It takes determination to keep walking with God and maintain a firm, unwavering purpose no matter what your circumstances dictate. The adoption process calls for a steadfast heart. You have to be intentional and trust God in the highs and lows of the journey. God uses the ones whose hearts are loyal and dedicated to Him. Stay confident in the Lord and keep a steadfast heart.

Baby Steps of Faith Personal Reflection

Psalm 57:7 My heart is steadfast, O God, my heart is steadfast; I will sing and make music.

Baby Step 45 – Is your heart steadfast?

Share your Story:

_____

_____

_____

_____

Trial or triumph? _____

Explain:

_____

_____

_____

_____

Personal Action Steps to Grow:

_____

_____

_____

_____

Supplication:

_____

_____

_____

_____

2 Peter 1:5-8 For this very reason, make every effort to add
to your faith goodness…knowledge…self-control…
perseverance…godliness…brotherly kindness…love.
For if you possess these qualities…they will keep you
from being ineffective and unproductive...

Barrenness is a painful and frustrating condition. It can take
on many forms – natural barrenness, financial, relational,
etc… It's anything in our lives as Christians that keeps us
from producing fruit. My personal relationship and walk
with Christ should result in fruit. God used my condition of
barrenness and the adoption process to produce fruit in me.
The "fruit" is Christ-like attitudes and behaviors. God did
the same thing through several women in the Bible.

Like Sarah, who had to die to her plan and stop trying to
make things happen. She learned to wait on the Lord with
faith and patience for the child God had promised her and
Abraham. (Genesis 18:13-14) Isaac, pleaded with the Lord,
in Rebekah's state of barrenness. They learned to pray
fervently. (Genesis 25:21) Rachel's barrenness revealed
several heart issues – envy, blaming others, strife, and
bitterness. God had to do a work in her heart first before
bringing the promise of a child. (Genesis 29:31) Hannah was
mocked by others since she was unable to bear a child and
found herself miserable and full of sorrow. She became hard
and bitter in her spirit because of her barrenness and
eventually her spiritual condition became a reflection of her
natural condition. God wanted to renew a right spirit in
Hannah. (1 Samuel 1:1-2)

Then came Elizabeth, an amazing woman of God. She did everything right and was still unable to bear fruit, in the sense of a child. Years passed and Elizabeth found herself too old to give birth. But her great faith proved that nothing's impossible with God. She taught us to trust God's timing.

Maybe you're like me and can identify with pieces of all of these woman. God wants to do a work in your hearts before He can fulfill the promise of a child. God wants you to enjoy a full and godly life. He also wants us to conduct ourselves like Christ and be transformed into His image. (2 Corinthians 3:18) That's the goal. Learn from these examples. Find strength as you wait like Sarah. Learn to pray fervently like Isaac and Rebekah. Yield to the Spirit like Rachel and spend time in God's presence and let go of envy, blame, and bitterness. Let God renew your heart. Get to the place where you believe nothing is impossible with God and trust His timing in bringing you the promised child, like Elizabeth.

2 Peter says if we possess these qualities we can and will be effective for the Lord. Live a life full of faith. Add to your faith – goodness, knowledge, perseverance, godliness, self-control, kindness, and love. When we surrender to God and allow real change to take place in our attitudes and behaviors – people notice. When we trust God in our painful and seemingly impossible situations, God shows up and makes a way, and others are drawn to Him through your story. We will be effective for the Lord and produce fruit – even in our barrenness.

Baby Steps of Faith Personal Reflection

2 Peter 1:5-8 For this very reason, make every effort to add
to your faith goodness…knowledge…self-control…
perseverance…godliness…brotherly kindness…love.
For if you possess these qualities…they will keep you
from being ineffective and unproductive…

Baby Step 46 – Are you producing fruit?

Share your Story:

_____
_____
_____
_____

Trial or triumph? _____

Explain:

_____
_____
_____
_____

Personal Action Steps to Grow:

_____
_____
_____
_____

Supplication:

_____
_____
_____
_____

Proverbs 31:25-28   She is clothed with strength and dignity; she can laugh at the days to come. She speaks with wisdom, and faithful instruction is on her tongue. She watches over the affairs of her household…her children arise and call her blessed; her husband also praises her.

Although I aspire to be the Proverbs 31 woman, there are numerous days I fall short. I read Proverbs 31 and quickly draw strength in knowing that I am a work in progress in the eyes of Jesus. Let's face it, when you're raising children, there are days you are barely clothed and in your right mind, much less *clothed with strength and dignity*. When my kids were younger, I was a "baby" Christian, not always representing the attitude of Christ, so lots of things rolled off my tongue. I'm certain it wasn't *faithful instruction.*

A Proverbs 31 woman watches over the affairs of her household. In other words, she checks off the following from her **TO DO LIST:**

Cook Meals – Clean House – Grocery Shop – Do Laundry – Pay Bills – PTA Meeting Homework Help – Soccer Practice – Pray for Kids – Plan Date Night – Cut Grass – Wash Car

Every morning my son would rise and call me "Mommy." I'm still waiting for him to call me *blessed!* Oddly enough, my *husband does praise me,* especially when I cut the grass and wash the car! I'm fairly sure that's not an accurate interpretation of the scripture.

I was thirty years old when I gave birth to our son Kyle and pushing forty when we adopted Makala. Today, I am fifty-four years old and writing a devotional to encourage you in your adoption process. My handsome son is twenty-four and my beloved adopted daughter is sixteen. I'm still a busy mother who watches over the affairs of her household and finding God every day in the ordinary. Because of my relationship with Jesus and spending time in God's Word, I believe I have gained some ground in the spiritual maturity department and have served the Lord many years in lots of different ministries. I love telling others about my Father God and how much He loves and cares for all of us. It's an honor and a privilege to speak into the lives of others through the scriptures, because those God-breathed words bring teaching, reproof, correction and training in righteousness. (2 Timothy 3:16) But the most gratifying portion is witnessing broken women become *clothed with strength and dignity* because of the love, hope, and trust they have in their everlasting Savior, Jesus.

If you're not already, one day soon, you'll be a mother. But you can start developing Proverbs 31 traits long before your child arrives. I serve with numerous young women at church. They are living examples of Christ in their speech, conduct, faith, love, and purity. Age does not reflect spiritual maturity. These young ladies keep me humble. Remember, it's a work in progress, both the adoption and becoming that Proverbs woman. It's a lofty goal. *She can laugh at the days ahead* – keep smiling, you got this.

Baby Steps of Faith Personal Reflection

Proverbs 31:25-28   She is clothed with strength and dignity;
she can laugh at the days to come. She speaks with wisdom,
and faithful instruction is on her tongue. She watches over
the affairs of her household…her children arise and call
her blessed; her husband also praises her.

Baby Step 47 – What Proverbs 31 trait challenges you most?

Share your Story:

_____

_____

_____

_____

Trial or triumph? _____

Explain:

_____

_____

_____

_____

Personal Action Steps to Grow:

_____

_____

_____

_____

Supplication:

_____

_____

_____

_____

Author Unknown

We are sitting at lunch one day when my daughter casually mentions that she and her husband are thinking of "starting a family."

We're taking a survey," she says half-joking. "Do you think I should have a baby?"

"It will change your life," I say, carefully keeping my tone neutral."

"I know," she says, "no more sleeping in on weekends, no more spontaneous vacations."

But that is not what I meant at all. I look at my daughter, trying to decide what to tell her. I want her to know what she will never learn in childbirth classes. I want to tell her that the physical wounds of child bearing will heal, but becoming a mother will leave her with an emotional wound so raw that she will forever be vulnerable.

I consider warning her that she will never again read a newspaper without asking, "What if that had been MY child?" That every plane crash, every house fire will haunt her; that when she sees pictures of starving children, she will wonder if anything could be worse than watching your child die.

I look at her carefully manicured nails and stylish suit and think that no matter how sophisticated she is, becoming a mother will reduce her to the primitive level of a bear protecting her cub. And that an urgent call of "Mom!" will cause her to drop a soufflé' or her best crystal without a moment's hesitation.

144

I feel I should warn her that no matter how many years she has invested in her career, she will be professionally derailed by motherhood. She might arrange for childcare, but one day she will be going to an important business meeting and she will think of her baby's sweet smell. She will have to use every ounce of discipline to keep from running home, just to make sure her baby is all right.

I want my daughter to know that every day decisions will no longer be routine. That a five year old boy's desire to go to the men's room rather than the women's at McDonald's will become a major dilemma. That right there, in the midst of clattering trays and screaming children, issues of independence and gender identity will be weighed against the prospect that a child molester may be lurking in that restroom.

However decisive she may be at the office, she will second-guess herself constantly as a mother. Looking at my attractive daughter, I want to assure her that eventually the needs of her child will come first and she will never feel the same about herself. That her life, now so important, will be of less value to her once she has a child. That she would give herself up in a moment to save her child, but will also begin to hope for more years, not accomplish her own dreams, but to watch her child accomplish theirs.

I want her to know that whatever scars or stretch marks she has earned in becoming a mother will now become badges of honor. My daughter's relationship with her husband will change, and not in the way she thinks. I wish she could understand how much more you can love a man who is careful to powder the baby or who never hesitates to play with his child. I think she should know that she will fall in love with him again for reasons we would now find very unromantic.

I wish my daughter could sense the bond she will feel with women throughout history who have tried to stop war, prejudice and drunk driving. I want to describe to my daughter the exhilaration of seeing your child learn to ride a bike. I want to capture for her the belly laugh of a baby who is touching the soft fur of a dog or cat for the first time. I want her to taste the joy that is so real it actually hurts.

My daughter's quizzical look makes me realize that tears have formed in my eyes. "You'll never regret it," I finally say. Then I reached across the table, squeezed my daughter's hand and offered a silent prayer for her, and for me, and for all the mere mortal women who stumble their way into this most wonderful of callings.

Baby Steps of Faith Personal Reflection

Motherhood – A Calling

Baby Step 48 – What touched you most in the Motherhood – A Calling story?

Share your Story:

_____

_____

_____

_____

Trial or triumph? _____

Explain:

_____

_____

_____

_____

Personal Action Steps to Grow:

_____

_____

_____

_____

Supplication:

_____

_____

_____

_____

Exodus 17:6 God speaking to Moses, "I will stand there
before you by the rock at Horeb. Strike the rock, and
water will come out of it for the people to drink."

Strike the rock and water will come out of it. Amazing isn't
it? What about the unbelievable burning bush story in
Exodus 3? *A bush was on fire, but it didn't burn up.* Well, I
don't have a rock or a bush, but I do have a peace lily. I
know, it's absolutely hilarious, but true. My story involves a
peace lily house plant that I received when my father died.
For years, whenever I found myself in a posture of seeking
God on a specific thing or direction in my life, within a few
days, my peace lily would bloom. Oddly enough, it always
bloomed the same way. A brand new shoot would emerge
from the center of the large plant and inevitably a beautiful
white lily would result. This went on for several years. It
may have been coincidence. If I were to consult a botanist, I
might discover that's how the peace lily blooms and it's not
that unusual, but that wouldn't explain the timing of those
blooms. God used a rock, a bush, fig tree, a donkey, and
even the north star to get the attention of His people. Why
not a peace lily?

It's harmless as long as one doesn't lose sight of the fact that
it's God trying to get my attention, right? When the peace
lily starts to impact my decisions, such as – two blooms
means "yes," three blooms means, "no," or I find myself in
deep desperation seeking out a bloom on the bloomless
plant in order to function daily, that may be a sign that I've
gotten things out of perspective. Let's say the plant dies and

I can't live without it! I've definitely lost perspective. Now, I have a false God on my hands!

Like Moses and the Israelites, I witnessed and benefited from many miracles on the adoption journey, but I could be so ungrateful and start complaining and grumbling within days of my breakthrough. I learned from the peace lily that God was with me in this difficult ordeal. God is so patient and continues to walk with us and provide, even as we complain. Moses struck the rock and God gave the Israelites water to drink. I woke up many mornings to a beautiful new peace lily right in the midst of my drought and like Moses, I sensed God standing there before me by the peace lily. God gave me peace that passes all human understanding with each bloom and reassured me that I was not alone on this journey.

Baby Steps of Faith Personal Reflection

Exodus 17:6 God speaking to Moses, "I will stand there before you by the rock at Horeb. Strike the rock, and water will come out of it for the people to drink."

Baby Step 49 – Is God using earthly things to get your attention?

Share your Story:

_____
_____
_____
_____

Trial or triumph? _____

Explain:

_____
_____
_____
_____

Personal Action Steps to Grow:

_____
_____
_____
_____

Supplication:

_____
_____
_____
_____

1 Corinthians 10:31 So whether you eat or drink or
whatever you do, do it all for the glory of God.

Timelines! Adoption is all about *TIME*. First, there's a ton of
paperwork, processing, and all of that takes *TIME*. Some of
these documents travel clear across cities, states, and even
countries all in a matter of *TIME*. They are handled, collated,
stamped, sealed, stuffed in large envelopes, and mailed from
one person to the next, more than you can imagine, and all
of that takes extra *TIME*.

These important papers see the desktops and countertops of
more official buildings and agencies than one would care to
count and all of that takes *TIME*. Unfortunately, mishaps
occur, and in the paper passing frenzy, documents are lost,
misplaced, or worse yet, never arrive. Inevitably, your
caseworker advises you to immediately redo necessary
procedures, retrieve new documents, and of course add
TIME to the process.

Whether you eat or drink, or whatever you do, do it all to
the glory of God. I have a few tips to help you use your
TIME wisely. Get a large binder and make several copies of
every piece of paper, document, certificate, etc... important
to your adoption process. File them alphabetically in the
binder and add tabs with a short description for quick
access. It's all about saving *TIME*. Keep ample gas in the car
for quick road trips to the nearest state capitol or federal
agency and always stay on friendly terms with your
neighborhood notary. All of these tips will help you save
TIME when those unfortunate mishaps occur. Last, but not

least, although this does not really affect minutes in your *TIME* sensitive adoption, it will certainly make the journey a bit more tolerable. Always have a plentiful supply of your favorite comfort food. For me, that was chocolate…lots of chocolate. I hope you have enough *TIME* to enjoy your favorite.

Be sure to make *TIME* for God in these adoption tasks and any other mundane daily activities like laundry and cooking meals. God loves it when we continually keep Him in the loop throughout our day. He loves being involved in all that we do and to do everything for His glory. You may not feel like these activities bring God a great deal of glory at the time, but in the grand scheme of things, they do make a difference in the lives of our family and especially, the life of one child you hope to one day call son or daughter. I find my day goes smoother in general when I spend time with the Lord first thing. If I do hit a snag, just knowing God is with me in the deal helps me maintain my course throughout the day. That's honoring Him in all that you do. Whether eating – drinking – sleeping – working – playing – filing adoption paperwork, give Him the credit for enabling you to get these ordinary tasks done *TIME* and *TIME* again and pass the chocolate.

Baby Steps of Faith Personal Reflection

1 Corinthians 10:31 So whether you eat or drink or whatever you do, do it all for the glory of God.

Baby Step 50 – How are you making TIME for God in the daily grind?

Share your Story:

_____
_____
_____
_____

Trial or triumph? _____

Explain:

_____
_____
_____
_____

Personal Action Steps to Grow:

_____
_____
_____
_____

Supplication:

_____
_____
_____
_____

1 Timothy 4:15-16 Be diligent in these matters; give
yourself wholly to them, so that everyone may see
your progress. Watch your life and doctrine
closely. Persevere in them, because if you do,
you will save both yourself and your hearers.

The entire chapter 4 of 1 Timothy is about being a good
minister of Jesus Christ. I am challenged each day to live this
out with family, friends, neighbors, co-workers, and those
involved in our adoption process. A minister makes sure
their life and conversation is like Jesus. That's easier said
than done. Some days you want to commit a felony, not
minister.

What a daunting task to be like Him who knew no sin,
perfect in every way. God knows we're not perfect, but He
wants us to live in the image of Christ and be like Him.
We're encouraged to watch our lives and doctrine closely.
We have to be mindful of the way we conduct ourselves
because people are watching. You may be the only Jesus
they ever meet.

There's a tremendous responsibility in being a minister. The
scripture says to persevere because if you do, you will save
both yourself and your hearers. Others are counting on us.
They are not only watching how we conduct our life, but
listening to how we speak. Is your tone of voice like Jesus?
Do you exercise patience and kindness in your words? Do
you walk and talk with humility? The New Living
Translation takes this poignant scripture and transforms it
into a simple checklist.

Be Like Jesus Checklist

- *Be diligent in these matters* – give your complete attention to these matters. Your life is your ministry. Ministry is hard work. Walk in integrity and be Jesus to people.

- *Give yourself wholly to them* – throw yourself into your tasks so everyone will see your progress. Spend time in prayer and worship. Go to church. Take bible studies. Attend conferences and cultivate the gifts God has given you.

- *Watch your life and doctrine closely* – Keep a close watch on how you live and what you're teaching. Take responsibility for your attitudes and actions. Seek wisdom and instruction from God's word. Correctly interpret the scriptures and seek the pastoral counsel when in doubt.

- *Persevere in them* – stay true to what is right and stay at it with no compromise. For me, persevere tells me it won't be easy, but it's worth the effort.

I'm not perfect, but I want my life to have purpose and make a difference for the gospel. Jesus gives me that desire. Jesus gives me the template. If you're adoption journey brought you to this devotional and it brought you closer to Jesus, then Paul was right in his instruction to Timothy *and me*. That we must persevere in these matters in order to save ourselves and others. It pays to stay diligent in our role as ministers of the gospel. You can do it.

Baby Steps of Faith Personal Reflection

1 Timothy 4:15-16 Be diligent in these matters; give yourself wholly to them, so that everyone may see your progress. Watch your life and doctrine closely. Persevere in them, because if you do, you will save both yourself and your hearers.

Baby Step 51 – What needs work on your checklist?

Share your Story:

_____
_____
_____
_____

Trial or triumph? _____

Explain:

_____
_____
_____
_____

Personal Action Steps to Grow:

_____
_____
_____
_____

Supplication:

_____
_____
_____
_____

Psalm 3:3 But you are a shield around me, O LORD;
you bestow glory on me and lift up my head.

After twenty months into the adoption process and still
waiting, it was difficult at times to lift our heads, but for the
shield around us. (Psalm 3:3) We continued to pray for favor
and the referral of a child from the beautiful Filipino
country. Our caseworker called to inform us that the Vice
President of our adoption agency, Lifelink, was planning to
travel to the Philippines in a few short weeks to visit several
orphanages and meet with the country's adoption directors.
The agency was planning to take the files of several waiting
families, including ours, to investigate the current delays in
referrals and overall placement of children from the
Philippines to the United States. We were really encouraged
to hear of the agency's travel plans, because just a few days
prior to this announcement, we inquired about the
possibility of receiving a case update specifically with the in-
country directors, and it didn't seem likely. Now, our case
was being hand delivered in-country by the Vice-President
of Lifelink Adoption Agency.

It was several weeks before our agency returned and spoke
with families seeking adoption in the Philippines.
Unfortunately, the Vice-President of the agency brought
back some unsettling news. Apparently, U.S. Immigration
was requiring the Philippines to complete additional
paperwork, described as quite extensive, so the Philippine
program decided at that point to place the majority of
available children in Australia and England. It could be done

quicker and with ease, which was beneficial for the waiting children. Placements would continue in the United States – but very limited. The weight of the world was on our shoulders.

Have you ever noticed how a distressing situation can cause you to become downcast? Your shoulders shrug, head hangs down, frowns take over smiles, and even your voice becomes a depressing tone. Discouragement and worry just take over your entire body. But over and over, God encourages us to *lift* our heads and hands to Him. God wants us to *lift* our eyes and shift our focus. He wants us to stop fixating on the problem and start seeing our blessings. Start seeing the answers to your prayers. Maybe your adoption process has added weight to your shoulders. Lift your eyes, shift your focus, and see your adopted child coming home. Continue to hold on to the vision and trust God. He's still in control. I know God wants to bless us abundantly. Let the words of the psalmist invade any distressing situation you may be encountering, "O Lord, you are a shield around me and the lifter of my head."

Baby Steps of Faith Personal Reflection

Psalm 3:3 But you are a shield around me, O LORD;
you bestow glory on me and lift up my head.

Baby Step 52 – What weight makes it tough to
lift your head?

Share your Story:

_____
_____
_____
_____

Trial or triumph? _____

Explain:

_____
_____
_____
_____

Personal Action Steps to Grow:

_____
_____
_____
_____

Supplication:

_____
_____
_____
_____

Baby Step 53

Baby Step 53   Closed Door

Proverbs 16:3 Commit to the LORD whatever
you do, and your plans will succeed.

The news of the Filipino program limiting U.S. placements left us a bit perplexed. After two years of waiting, it appeared that we had no other choice, but to continue waiting until a Filipino child was referred or the door to this country was completely shut. Generally, a closed door can lead to great disappointment and frustration, especially when you've been waiting and trusting God for such a long time. Adopting parents usually come to terms early on in the process that placement of a child may not happen instantly. They simply start walking the adoption road. There are many paths that lead to many agencies and children, but they must choose one. Once they decide which agency, perhaps a country, they begin to head that direction and invest everything they have physically, financially, emotionally, spiritually – only to get within a stone's throw and see the door close. Closed doors can 1. Redirect you – lead you to another door 2. Cause you to regroup – take a break and have a Gatorade, regain momentum and push the existing door harder 3. Quit – self explanatory 4. Wait – let God show Himself good.

My husband and I had committed this adoption to the Lord and He promised the plan would succeed. Quitting was not an option. God called us to adopt and we were determined to complete the task. A closed door is not always a bad thing; it can lead you to better things. It can force you to change your direction and ultimately lead you to the right

160

door. Our agency choose to push the door harder and continually faxed the Filipino directors and requested information on future referrals, but heard nothing back. We choose to wait and let God show Himself good and that's exactly what happened next. Our adoption agency graciously offered to put us at the top of the Korean placement list. God was opening another door and in the most unexpected way. God does not want to withhold good things from us. (Psalm 84:11) God wants to show Himself good. I encourage you to commit to the Lord in whatever you do and your plans will succeed. Are doors closing around you? Let Him work it out. Ask Him to give you patience in the wait and trust Him. Something better is in the works and when that door opens you will walk right into the blessing.

Baby Steps of Faith Personal Reflection

Proverbs 16:3 Commit to the LORD whatever
you do, and your plans will succeed.

Baby Step 53 – Any closed doors?

Share your Story:

_____
_____
_____
_____

Trial or triumph? _____

Explain:

_____
_____
_____
_____

Personal Action Steps to Grow:

_____
_____
_____
_____

Supplication:

_____
_____
_____
_____

Deuteronomy 28:1-2 If you fully obey the LORD your
God and carefully follow all his commands…all
these blessings will come upon you and accompany
you if you obey the LORD your God.

Each day I pray this devotional strengthens, encourages, and inspires you to pursue adoption with all your heart. I hope it also stirs in you the desire to fully obey the Lord your God, follow His commands, and experience His countless blessings on your life. Our adoption took place sixteen years ago. Although it was challenging, I have no regrets. I would travel that road all over again today. I fell more in love with Jesus, healed and restored broken areas of my life, learned valuable spiritual truths that continue to help me live victoriously, and received the blessing of a child. The latter is truly *the moment* when all of God's blessing comes upon you and overtakes you. However, years later – after the adoption, I learned a valuable spiritual truth on releasing the blessings of God into our lives. You don't want to go another day on your journey without this revelation.

Unfortunately, we live most of our lives dependent upon our feelings and circumstances instead of living by faith. A blessing is words spoken over something or someone and they're good words. God set before us life and death, blessings and curses. Your words have the ability to produce life or death, blessings and curses. God told us to choose life, but it's our choice. You choose by the words you declare. It's up to us to release the blessings into our life – they come out of our mouth! Our words reveal our faith. So many times, my words revealed the negative thoughts of my situation. Many times my words were worrisome, full of doubt and fear. I often grumbled and complained and declared I was miserably forgotten by God. Our pastor repeatedly tells the congregation, "Every member, every day, in God's Word." Why? Because when you spend time reading and meditating on the scriptures, it will change how you think and speak. When we speak what we believe, backed by the Word of God, we are making a confession. Make a list of confessions, note scriptural promises tailored to your situations, and declare them over your life, your family, your circumstances, and your future. Personalize them as you speak them aloud. "God has a plan for Brenda, hope and a future." (Jeremiah 29:11) *The written word, becomes the spoken word, becomes the living word.* Acting on this spiritual truth, will release blessings into your life and adoption. Start confessing the Word of God.

Baby Steps of Faith Personal Reflection

Deuteronomy 28:1-2 If you fully obey the LORD your God and carefully follow all his commands…all these blessings will come upon you and accompany you if you obey the LORD your God.

Baby Step 54 – What are you confessing?

Share your Story:

_____
_____
_____
_____

Trial or triumph? _____

Explain:

_____
_____
_____
_____

Personal Action Steps to Grow:

_____
_____
_____
_____

Supplication:

_____
_____
_____
_____

Hebrews 11:1 Now faith is being sure of what we
hope for and certain of what we do not see.

I aspire to live a life of faith. Faith is being sure of what we
hope for and certain of what we do not see. Hebrews 11 is
filled with stories of faith-filled men and women. Those that
seemingly had that unquestionable belief and utter
obedience to the Father. I find I am more like the father of
the boy with convulsions who said to Jesus, "I believe, but
help my unbelief." (Mark 9:24) My faith isn't always perfect
and despite what it seems, I bet these great Old Testament
Faith Heroes had moments similar to mine.

Remember the God-given dream and my sweet friend
Kelly's message to our family? How could one forget
something so unbelievable, right? God told Kelly that when
the news of her baby's arrival was shared with others, so
would our child be born. Faith sees the unseen. God is
unseen, but I still believe. There was no certainty that our
baby was going to be born in March. We knew nothing
about the child God had for our family except that she
would be a girl. We would have a daughter. But our
amazing God brought a message to us through a dear friend.
Our babies would be born in the spring. Faith is being
convinced that whatever God says it's good and true. You
can count on it.

Faith is the title deed of our hopes and dreams. We don't see
them. Our hopes and dreams have not been fulfilled, but we
believe and act with relentless assurance that somehow,
someway God will do it. I believe these bible heroes – Noah,

Abraham, Moses – all saw something in the spirit. Each one of them had a vision, a picture, on the inside of them that God painted and they were certain of the promise of God. It was a faith picture. My friend had stirred my spirit with her announcement of a new child and her dream about my child. God used her to give me a faith picture. I pictured my child being born in the spring and arriving home shortly thereafter.

God gave Abraham a faith picture. He took him outside and said, "Look up at the heavens and count the stars – if indeed you can count them." Then he said to him, "So shall your offspring be." God had Abraham look up at the sky and gave him a faith picture that he could relate to. God gave Abraham a promise and it gave him hope. God did the same thing in my life in giving a wonderful dream to a friend, who had faith enough to believe, and shared it with me. Abraham and I both believed the Lord would fulfill our hopes and dreams. Over the years my faith has grown. I long to know God's will and spend time in the scriptures. God is looking to and fro for people of faith. (2 Chronicles 16:9) I want to be that person. How about you?

The time had come and the dream was fulfilled. Joshua Bryce was born March 19, 1998. With the birth of our friend's son, we knew *by faith* that our Korean daughter's birth had also taken place. Most children are placed within six months of their birthday – news would be coming soon. Faith is being sure of what you hope for and certain of what you can not see. Look up at the stars and let a faith picture stir in your heart – your dream of a child fulfilled.

Baby Steps of Faith Personal Reflection

Hebrews 11:1 Now faith is being sure of what we
hope for and certain of what we do not see.

Baby Step 55 – Do you have a faith picture?

Share your Story:

_____

_____

_____

_____

Trial or triumph? _____

Explain:

_____

_____

_____

_____

Personal Action Steps to Grow:

_____

_____

_____

_____

Supplication:

_____

_____

_____

_____

1 Thessalonians 5:16-18 Be joyful always; pray
continually; give thanks in all circumstances,
for this is God's will for you in Christ Jesus.

There are only two phone calls you genuinely look forward
to as adopting parents. The first call is the referral of your
child to include a picture and paperwork. The second call is
traveling details and a sure sign your child is coming home.
It was a typical hot summer day when we received the first
of these two very important phone calls. Our caseworker
had received the paperwork of a little girl born in Kyunngi-
do, South Korea on April 15, 1998. Immediately, we noted
her birthday. She was born three weeks after Joshua Bryce. It
came to pass, just as God had told my friend Kelly in a
dream. *"When the news of your baby's arrival is shared
with others, your friend's child will also be born."* God is so
amazing!

This precious little baby was named Myung Ok Han. She
was three months old. A meeting was scheduled the
following day to view her photo and discuss the details. It
was happening! As I hung up the phone, all I could think to
do was get down on my knees and thank God. My heart was
over-flowing with gratitude and joy. After two years of
waiting on the Lord, we were suddenly moving forward and
walking into our blessing.

A thankful heart is so important. We need to be thankful to
God in all circumstances…for all things. I admit, I'm not
always grateful or joyful in all things. Sometimes I don't like
what I'm going through or how it feels and joy is all but

elusive in the trials of this life; yet, God tells us to be joyful always. No matter what your situation, God requires us to be joyful. The joy of the Lord is my strength. (Nehemiah 8:10) What brings real joy? The people of Israel were encouraged to eat, drink and be joyful after they heard the law of the Lord. They wept in repentance and broke into fellowship together. This tells me the joy of the Lord is continually staying in close relationship with the Lord. Read the Bible. Pray regularly. Go to church. Do the right thing. Fellowship with other believers to encourage one another. This is how we overcome and keep our joy in the midst of difficult times. Bible greats endured many trials and continued to give God praise and thanksgiving because they knew He was faithful. They trusted God with their situation. Remember, God is for us and not against us. (Romans 8:28) That alone is a reason to be joyful.

Like Hannah, I prayed for this child, and the Lord granted me what I asked of Him and I worshipped the Lord there in that place. (1 Samuel) I fell to my knees and worshipped Him right in the middle of my kitchen. God heard Hannah's cries, he heard mine, and he hears your prayers for a child. No matter what you're facing today, I pray the joy of the Lord is your strength and you're able to give God thanks for more than one thing in your life. Be joyful, pray continually, and give thanks in all circumstances for this is God's will for you in Christ Jesus.

Baby Steps of Faith Personal Reflection

1 Thessalonians 5:16-18 Be joyful always; pray
continually; give thanks in all circumstances,
for this is God's will for you in Christ Jesus.

Baby Step 56 – What portion of 1 Thessalonians 5:16-18 challenges you?

Share your Story:

_____
_____
_____
_____

Trial or triumph? _____

Explain:

_____
_____
_____
_____

Personal Action Steps to Grow:

_____
_____
_____
_____

Supplication:

_____
_____
_____
_____

> Isaiah 58:6 Is not this the kind of fasting I have chosen:
> to loose the chains of injustice and untie the cords
> of the yoke, to set the oppressed free and break
> every yoke?

I engaged in many spiritual disciplines during the adoption process and still do as a believer in Jesus. I attended church service regularly, read the scriptures, attended bible studies and prayed continually. However, there's one spiritual discipline that I neglected during our adoption process, but have recently found very beneficial, and that is fasting. Fasting is the most powerful spiritual discipline. In a fast, a follower of Christ chooses to do without something that is hard to do without. Biblical fasting usually involved abstaining from food. However, if there's something in your life that "eats up" a lot of your time and keeps you from being fully devoted to God, it may be time to call a fast. Maybe it's too much television, cell phone usage, time spent on the internet/social media, hobbies, exercising, shopping, music, books – all of which can easily consume a person. It controls us and too much of anything is not a good thing. It's important to maintain balance in your life.

Hunger for God and feast at His table. Set aside a certain amount of time – a few days, a week, a month - pray and spend time in the scriptures in place of these other activities. Jesus fasted for forty days. If Jesus had to set aside time to draw closer to His father in fasting and prayer, I think we ought to consider this important. The bible tells us Moses, King David, and many great men and women of the Bible fasted and prayed because it was beneficial in their walk with God.

Adoption is a big decision. It's not for the weak at heart. Here are some of the benefits of fasting before and during your adoption process. There will be numerous decisions and you'll need wisdom. Fasting clears your mind, makes you sensitive to the Holy Spirit and enables you to hear from God. Opposition will come and you will need to be steadfast and determined. Fasting unleashes the kind of power to help you stand and keep standing. It could be a long journey and you will grow weary in the wait. You'll need renewed strength and hope. Fasting stirs your faith and renews your strength and hope in God. You will need God's help. Fasting causes you to humble yourself before God and demonstrate your need for Him in your life and in this new endeavor, your calling, and ministry.

I was not a mature Christian when we started the adoption process. There were numerous challenges and because of God's unfailing love, patience and grace I grew through those challenges; but, fasting regularly could have eliminated troubled areas of my life much sooner and would have unleashed a supernatural power to help me in my time of need. For years, I struggled with negative thoughts, feelings of inferiority, comparison traps, endless worry and on and on. Isaiah 58:6 demonstrates the power of fasting. It breaks the yoke and sets the oppressed free. Fasting invites the supernatural power of God into your life and ushers in breakthrough and miracles. The benefits of fasting far outweigh the costs. Make a sacrificial choice to skip some meals or set aside time consuming activities in order to draw closer to God. You will experience God in a whole new way.

Baby Steps of Faith Personal Reflection

Isaiah 58:6 Is not this the kind of fasting I have chosen:
to loose the chains of injustice and untie the cords
of the yoke, to set the oppressed free and break
every yoke?

Baby Step 57 – For spiritual benefits,
what would you consider fasting?

Share your Story:

_____

_____

_____

_____

Trial or triumph? _____

Explain:

_____

_____

_____

_____

Personal Action Steps to Grow:

_____

_____

_____

Supplication:

_____

_____

_____

_____

Galatians 3:28 There is neither Jew nor Greek, slave
nor free, male nor female, for you are all
one in Christ Jesus.

With much excitement and anticipation we looked forward
to meeting with our caseworker to review Makala's referral
paperwork and photo. After two years of waiting, we were
just hours from seeing the face of our new baby daughter
from Korea. Until a few months ago, I imagined the face of a
Filipino child, but once the agency put us on the Korean list,
I began to spend hours searching websites and thumbing
through adoption brochures viewing pictures of Korean
children. I discovered my new baby from Korea was going
to look a lot different than me. I shamefully admit that I was
struggling with some of those differences. If I was
struggling, would others in our extended family struggle?
What was suppose to be the most amazing day, was being
polluted by my thinking – just as Paul warned. (James 1:27)
But God is all merciful and full of grace, slow to anger, and
rich in love. (Psalm 145:8)

*Webster defines discrimination – the practice of unfairly
treating a person or group of people differently from
other people or groups of people*

Now that I had discovered the differences, I had a choice to
make. How would I respond to those differences? Would I
discriminate? How would I let them affect my thinking…my
heart…my actions? Unknowingly, my seven year old son
Kyle and the Holy Spirit lead me ever so gently through this
lesson on wholeheartedly embracing one's differences as our

meeting unfolded. Our caseworker reached into the file and pulled out Makala's picture. She held it face down, close to her chest, announcing that Kyle would be the first one to see her precious little face. She then handed it to Kyle. With absolutely no hesitation in his voice, his face and eyes lit up the room and proudly he announced, "Oh she's so cute. She's *just* so cute. She's my sister. Now, when is she coming home?"

Are you struggling with your child looking different from you? Maybe you purposely didn't choose to adopt a child who looks different because you knew it would pose challenges and you weren't sure how to scale the dividing wall. It's simple. Choose to **break down the dividing wall** just like Paul instructed in Ephesus. (Ephesians 2:13-14) There is neither Jew nor Greek, slave now free, male nor female, Asian or Caucasian, Black or Hispanic, Vietnamese or Chinese, for we are all one in Christ. See people with the eyes of Christ as Kyle did that day. We're all **one body** in Jesus.

Baby Steps of Faith Personal Reflection

Galatians 3:28 There is neither Jew nor Greek, slave
nor free, male nor female, for you are all
one in Christ Jesus.

Baby Step 58 – Do you struggle with race
or ethnic differences?

Share your Story:

_____
_____
_____
_____

Trial or triumph? _____

Explain:

_____
_____
_____
_____

Personal Action Steps to Grow:

_____
_____
_____
_____

Supplication:

_____
_____
_____
_____

Isaiah 35:10 ...and those the LORD has rescued will return. They will enter Zion with singing; everlasting joy will crown their heads. Gladness and joy will overtake them, and sorrow and sighing will flee away.

There is no other verse that best describes the day a child is matched to your family. In fact, when I read all ten verses of Chapter 35 it's as if they were penned for that very moment. In the Old Testament this chapter describes the people coming out of sin and judgment right into the arms of Almighty God. Isaiah also prophesizes the coming of Jesus in this chapter. It's a mega celebration! Allow me to translate...

Verse 1:2 - The desert and the parched land will be glad; the wilderness will rejoice and blossom. Like the crocus, it will burst into bloom; it will rejoice greatly and shout for joy. God delivered me out of my dry and unsatisfying desert to a new place in full bloom. Your wilderness will bloom when you allow the living water into your wasteland. Today a baby girl bloom would burst forth – born April 15, 1998 in South Korea.

Verse 3-4 - Strengthen the feeble hands, steady the knees that give way; say to those with fearful hearts, Be strong, do not fear; your God will come. He will come to save you. Dear friend, let our day of rejoicing in receiving the news that a child was matched to our family encourage you and steady your knees that God is continually working on the details of your adoption. Be strong and do not fear.

Verse 6-7 - Water will gush forth in the wilderness and streams in the desert. The burning sand will become a pool, the thirsty ground bubbling springs. In the haunts where jackals once lay, grass and reeds and papyrus will grow. God used the wilderness to draw me closer to Him. Because of His loving kindness, mercy, and patience my landscape changed inside (heart and mind) and outside (attitudes and behaviors) for His glory.

Verse 8-9 - And a highway will be there; it will be called the Way of Holiness. The unclean will not journey on it; it will be for those who walk in that Way; wicked fools will not go about on it. Most roads in Isaiah's day were dangerous trails and traveler's were vulnerable. But Isaiah describes a highway that is completely safe and available to God's redeemed people. You can only get there through Jesus Christ. You are on the right road my friend. Taking Jesus on your adoption journey was smart. He is the Way and He knows the way. I am confident you will get to the finish line.

Verse 10 - Therefore the redeemed of the Lord will return to Zion with singing; everlasting joy will crown their heads. Gladness and joy will overtake them, and sorrow and sighing will flee away. Thank God for the redemption we have through Jesus. He's a faithful, good God. Thank God for Makala. Gladness and joy did overtake our family on this wonderful day. Like the people of Zion, we were thankful for God's blessing. Continue walking your path for I am confident that God will lead you to Zion where everlasting joy will crown your head.

Baby Steps of Faith Personal Reflection

Isaiah 35:10 ...and those the LORD has rescued will return. They will enter Zion with singing; everlasting joy will crown their heads. Gladness and joy will overtake them, and sorrow and sighing will flee away.

Baby Step 59 – What portion of this verse ministers most to you?

Share your Story:

_____
_____
_____
_____

Trial or triumph? _____

Explain:

_____
_____
_____
_____

Personal Action Steps to Grow:

_____
_____
_____
_____

Supplication:

_____
_____
_____
_____

Psalm 19:1 The heavens declare the glory of God; the
skies proclaim the work of His hands.

One December our family took a trip to Colorado. We
planned a wonderful snowmobile adventure. I remember as
we ascended the mountain, the beauty of the fresh fallen
snow and the tall evergreens filling the air with their
masculine scent. The skies displayed the deepest of blue. It
was majestic and I praised God inside of myself at the work
of His hands. Our God is indeed creative.

Now, it was time to let our creative juices flow and share
some very exciting news. We formally accepted Myung Ok
Han as our daughter! (July, 1998) Finally, we were able to
put the precious face of our child to *thee name* we had
chosen just for her – *Makala Myung.* Kyle was more than
ready to share the news of becoming a big brother with
family, friends, and neighbors. We took great care in visiting
everyone and presented them with what appeared to be a
gift. It was a framed picture of Makala. At times it was
presented gift wrapped and other times in a gift bag. All of
which was in the back seat of our car and part of the fun as
we drove from home to home. We couldn't risk this amazing
news getting out before we got to everyone; so, we appealed
to those who had been surprised, *to keep the surprise*, and
made our rounds all the same day. It was incredibly fun to
watch everyone open the frame, study intently the photo of
this precious little Korean baby in a pink sleeper, and finally
make the connection. It always lead to shouting, hugging,
and a crying frenzy. Kyle was loving every moment and I

felt so wonderfully blessed as I witnessed so much love and compassion in every household. Our family and friends had made room in their hearts for this little child from another place in the world. They endured the highs and lows with us for over two years. It was happening. The day all of us had been waiting for had arrived and it was time to celebrate.

Be creative and have fun introducing your child's photo to family and friends. There are no family phone calls announcing your water's broke and you're heading to the hospital to deliver your baby, however, you can be spontaneous and capture the element of surprise in your adoption. Today, there are more ideas at your fingertips with Facebook, Pinterest and Instagram. Introducing your child via a referral photograph is a really big day for the adopting family. Be original and let God's creative hand flow through you.

Baby Steps of Faith Personal Reflection

Psalm 19:1 The heavens declare the glory of God; the skies proclaim the work of His hands.

Baby Step 60 – Any creative referral photo sharing ideas?

Share your Story:

_____
_____
_____
_____

Trial or triumph? _____

Explain:

_____
_____
_____
_____

Personal Action Steps to Grow:

_____
_____
_____
_____

Supplication:

_____
_____
_____
_____

Philippians 2:3 Do nothing out of selfish ambition or
vain conceit, but in humility consider others better
than yourselves.

Days after sharing the news with family and friends, I found
myself reading and re-reading Makala's paperwork. It just
seemed surreal after such a long wait to have a picture and
actual information about our child. She was born in
Kyunggi-do, South Korea on April 15, 1998. She weighed 4
pounds and 16.7 inches long. She arrived earlier than
expected and was incubated for three days, but she thrived.
She had dark hair and eyes and medium skin color. The
information was not extensive, but helped us put together
her tapestry, one thread at a time. My friend Trischa, who is
also a parent of adoption, would talk about life in the form
of a tapestry. If you were to look carefully at a tapestry, you
would find one side full of threads, woven together, but it
doesn't really look like much on that particular side.
However, when you turn it over, you discover a
masterpiece. A beautiful tapestry created by a lifetime of
threads, each representing a life that has touched yours,
woven together, creating your masterpiece…your life.

One very important thread in Makala's tapestry was her
birth mother, Woo Ree Han. She was 15 years old when she
gave birth to Makala. In her third year of school, she realized
she was pregnant and unable to care for a baby. The agency
informed us that it's highly unusual for the family to
support a young girl in this condition in the Korean culture.
Woo Ree Han would have to make a difficult decision and

put her child up for adoption. What a selfless act of love and bravery. To put others first is a noble gesture. Whether or not she knew Jesus, she demonstrated Christ in her selfless act of putting her child's interest and welfare above her own. This is an example of one who has the mind of Christ.

Do you have the mind of Christ when you consider the birth mother in your adoption process? No matter what you know or don't know about this woman, God still commands us to this instruction. Are you counting her more significant than yourself? Maybe you don't think she deserves it? Christ died on the cross for me and I know I did not serve it; but, He did it anyway. If you're unable to see your child's birthmother with the mind of Christ, I want to encourage you to start seeing her differently. God wants us to extend grace, be humble, and strive for oneness in all relationships. This command includes the birth mother of your child. Pray for her daily and count her significant.

I am forever grateful to Woo Ree Han for the life she gave to my child. Her selfless act changed the course of my life forever and her thread is woven not only in Makala's tapestry, but my own. As fate would have it, the day I penned these notes about Woo Ree Han in my journal, this profound quote was shared in my morning bible study.

"Every noble life leaves its fiber interwoven forever in the work of the world."

Baby Steps of Faith Personal Reflection

Philippians 2:3 Do nothing out of selfish ambition or vain conceit, but in humility consider others better than yourselves.

Baby Step 61 – How do you see your child's birth mother?

Share your Story:

_____
_____
_____
_____

Trial or triumph? _____

Explain:

_____
_____
_____
_____

Personal Action Steps to Grow:

_____
_____
_____
_____

Supplication:

_____
_____
_____
_____

Joel 2:25 I will repay you for the years the locusts
have eaten...

The most familiar passage in Joel is God's promise of
restoration. In Joel 2:25-26 God promised to restore or
replace the years the locust had eaten. You have to
understand the impact of this promise. You see the entire
land of Judah suffered under a massive locust plague that
resulted in failed crops, dead livestock, and the death of
many people. It's amazing sometimes what God has to allow
in our lives in order to get our attention and bring us to
repentance. But that same God wants to bring restoration to
our devastation. He wants to restore *the years* the locusts
have eaten.

There were years where I willingly allowed the locusts to eat
away at my life through unwholesome talk and bitterness
towards lots of people. I nursed jealousy and felt very
entitled to my anger. I would participate in gossip and
slander. These locusts accompanied me through some dark
days of barrenness and even through the adoption process.
Joel urged the people to repent and encouraged them that
God truly wanted to restore the devastation left behind by
the locusts. Repentance is simply apologizing to God for
your actions. A heart-felt confession recognizes the sin and
sincerely asks forgiveness. Go to the Lord and keep it
honest. He is a gracious God and slow to anger. (v.13) He
will forgive and bless your life.

Part of the restoration process may include apologizing not
only to the Lord, but to some people you have hurt along the

way. Imagine that? I know from personal experience that I harbored bitterness against many innocent people. They actually tried to help, but I was too full of pride and it was easier to gossip than admit my faults. The most devastating locust damage was jealousy and anger towards every woman who had what I so desperately wanted – a child. Some of these woman took residence within my own family. I felt so ashamed and guilty for feeling the way I did. I wasted so many valuable years. Pray and ask God if you need to write a note or a letter asking forgiveness. He'll show you what to do and the grace to walk it out. It's worth it.

Whatever has been lost in your life, I pray that the book of Joel will remind you that God is a God of restoration. He is able to restore what has been stolen from you. The Land of Judah would eat in plenty, they would be satisfied, and praise the name of the Lord who had dealt wondrously with them. And God promised that His people would never be put to shame. Allow God to deal wondrously with you. Turn and keep coming back to the Lord with all your heart until every hindrance is removed and the brokenness restored. He will give back more than you can imagine in your life, within your heart, and your quiver.

Baby Steps of Faith Personal Reflection

Joel 2:25 I will repay you for the years the locusts
have eaten…

*Baby Step 62 – What locusts have you allowed
to eat away at your life?*

Share your Story:

_____
_____
_____
_____

Trial or triumph? _____

Explain:

_____
_____
_____
_____

Personal Action Steps to Grow:

_____
_____
_____
_____

Supplication:

_____
_____
_____
_____

Hebrews 12:2 Let us fix our eyes on Jesus, the
author and perfector of our faith…

Makala's acceptance paperwork was mailed July, 1998 to the
Korean agency. Her arrival was scheduled for October or
November. It was mid-November and our precious
daughter was still not able to take residence in her forever
home. There was no news and no explanation for the delay.
There are some days in the adoption process you simply file
under - STANDARD PROCEDURE.

Your heart skips a beat every time the phone rings. Could
this be the day? It had to be soon as our projected arrival
time was upon us. All that said, our caseworker finally
called and informed us that Korea would not be issuing
passports to travelers who had not cleared processing by
October 31. The government virtually shuts down for a two
month holiday at the end of each year. Really? The agency
was not sure if Makala's passport had been processed prior
to the deadline, but the fact that we were into mid-
November, indicated a strong probability that it *did not*
clear in time. It looked as though we would have to wait and
see – STANDARD PROCEDURE.

Our October arrival was but an illusion. Thanksgiving had
come and gone. It was mid-December and Makala's
Christmas stocking hung on the mantle for the third year,
but no Makala. She was now eight months old. The agency
called and confirmed that her passport did not process and
her estimated time of arrival would be late January or early
February – STANDARD PROCEDURE.

We were missing so much precious time with our baby. Christmas gifts had been purchased for Makala. At this point, I think the extended family took it harder than we did and that was noteworthy. God was perfecting our faith. If ever there was a time to "fix our eyes on Jesus" this was it. Perfect faith is the kind of faith that rests. It's the kind of faith that knows and is confident in God's plan no matter what it looks like or how long it takes. You maintain your peace and wait for the promise – STANDARD PROCEDURE.

I love the chorus to a song by Keith and Kristy Getty that beautifully illustrates my point and how we had grown in and through the adoption process.

We will stand as children of the promise,
We will fix our eyes on Him our soul's reward.
Till the race is finished and the work is done,
We'll walk by faith and not by sight.

Keep trusting and standing on the promises –

STANDARD PROCEDURE

Baby Steps of Faith Personal Reflection

Hebrews 12:2 Let us fix our eyes on Jesus, the
author and perfector of our faith...

Baby Step 63 – What is STANDARD PROCEDURE for you today?

Share your Story:

_____
_____
_____
_____

Trial or triumph? _____

Explain:

_____
_____
_____
_____

Personal Action Steps to Grow:

_____
_____
_____
_____

Supplication:

_____
_____
_____
_____

Matthew 1:23 The virgin will be with child and will give
birth to a son, and they will call him Immanuel – which
means, "God with us."

Let's take a walk down *Memory Lane*…

- Christmas 1996 – I discovered my husband writing a
  letter to our adopted daughter. She had not yet been
  born; but God knew her before she was formed in her
  mother's womb. God knew we would answer the call
  to adopt and in time His promise would be fulfilled in
  our lives.

- Christmas 1997 – I purchased a stocking for Makala
  and placed it on the mantle along with everyone in
  the family. I would write a letter this year to our
  unborn child and continue to water the seed that God
  had sown in our hearts.

- Christmas 1998 – You continue to reside in our hearts
  and your baby picture stands tall in a Christmas
  frame; but, you didn't make it home. The tree is
  adorned with twinkling lights, gifts for you are under
  the tree and your stocking adorns the mantle. We will
  wait until you come home…January…February…

There's still a reason to celebrate. The virgin will be with
child and will give birth to a son, and they will call Him
Immanuel, which means, "God with us." In spite of our
longing to have you home this Christmas, we celebrate that
God made His home among us. He never leaves us or
forsakes us. He is with us day and night; in good times and

bad; valleys and the mountaintops. Yesterday, today, and tomorrow – *Immanuel* – God is with us. You may not have come to live with us this Christmas sweet Makala; but, God came through the birth of Jesus to dwell among us and to live right where we do and that's worth celebrating!

The Lord Jesus was given many names throughout the New Testament – Light of the World, the Lamb of God, the Bread of Life, Christ the Savior, Rose of Sharon, The Bright Morning Star to name a few. Each name uniquely reflected His character and strength. None brings more comfort to my heart, especially today, than Immanuel – God is with us. It was a day to keep our eyes fixed on the Savior of the World and set our hearts on the baby in the manger. Thank you God for your indescribable gift…Jesus.

Baby Steps of Faith Personal Reflection

Matthew 1:23 The virgin will be with child and will give birth to a son, and they will call him Immanuel – which means, "God with us."

Baby Step 64 – How does Immanuel – God is with us – affect your circumstances?

Share your Story:

_____
_____
_____
_____

Trial or triumph? _____

Explain:

_____
_____
_____
_____

Personal Action Steps to Grow:

_____
_____
_____
_____

Supplication:

_____
_____
_____
_____

2 Corinthians 12:9-10 But he said to me, "My grace
is sufficient for you, for my power is made perfect
in weakness."

Can you hear "Auld Lang Syne" playing in the background?
Christmas had come and gone and everyone was enjoying
some down time before ringing in the New Year. We have
not heard any news from our agency since mid-December
when they confirmed that Makala did not make the
processing deadline of October 31, 1998. That pushed her
arrival to late January or early February. I am trying to
remain strong, but growing weak.

Paul had an amazing perspective. He said, "I will boast all
the more gladly about my weaknesses, so that Christ's
power may rest on me. For when I am weak, then I am
strong." Paul was talking about those moments when you
absolutely cannot make it through in your own strength.
Those moments when you cannot stand, so you lean on
Jesus. That would best describe my position during these
last few months of waiting for Makala to come home. I was
running on empty. But Jesus said, "My grace is sufficient."
Grace is undeserving favor and sufficient is enough to meet
a need or purpose. This verse means that no matter what
your going through as long as you lean on Jesus everything
will be fine. He will provide whatever you need to get
through. Are you running on empty in your adoption
process? You're going to make it. His power is made perfect
in your weakness. In other words, God is refueling your
tank to keep you going to the finish line. You can't do it in

your own strength but by God's grace and strength you can and will do it!

None of my resources, connections, time, money, abilities, or anything else was going to change our child's homecoming or lighten my load in the process. Nothing else but leaning on the greatness of God. I was determined to resist the temptation to respond in fear, anger, despair or frustration. I want to encourage you to do the same and call on the Lord when you feel weak or limited. God's strength is made great in the midst of our weaknesses. Remember Paul would boast in his weaknesses. Why? Because He knew in that moment, the power of Christ would rest on him and help him get through the difficult time. God's presence can transform you in the midst of your negative situation. Paul turned his into an opportunity to praise God. I do remember saying to family and friends during the last few months, "God knows what he's doing and if he needs more time to bring our baby home, so be it." Clearly that was a statement from a woman who was not speaking in her own strength, but walking in the all sufficient grace that Paul experienced many times in his ministry and declared that day to the Corinthians. God's grace is enough to get you through. You're stronger than you think.

Baby Steps of Faith Personal Reflection

2 Corinthians 12:9-10 But he said to me, "My grace is sufficient for you, for my power is made perfect in weakness."

Baby Step 65 – Any weak spots?

Share your Story:

_____

_____

_____

_____

Trial or triumph? _____

Explain:

_____

_____

_____

_____

Personal Action Steps to Grow:

_____

_____

_____

_____

Supplication:

_____

_____

_____

_____

Exodus 14:16, 18   Raise your staff and stretch out your hand
over the sea to divide the water so that the Israelites can
go through...they will know that I am Lord.

Kyle and I were enjoying the holidays immensely. I decided
to take him to see the movie *Prince of Egypt.* It's a great
story about Moses, who when you think about it, was more
or less adopted. Moses was born to an Israelite family, but
because Pharaoh had ordered every baby boy to be thrown
in the Nile, his mother hid him for three months. Then, she
placed him in a basket and sent it floating down the Nile
River. His sister Miriam stood at a distance watching what
became of her baby brother. The basket was discovered by
Pharaoh's daughter and to make a long story short, she
raised Moses as an Egyptian, knowing all the while he was
Hebrew, an Israelite. Women will go to great lengths for a
child. Can you relate?

The film depicted so many faith-filled miraculous moments
in the life of Moses. There was Moses and the burning bush.
Then God displayed His awesome power when he turned
the staff of Moses into a snake. How about when he turned
his hand leprous and then back to healthy flesh again? Let's
not forget when the Nile turned to blood. The story of Moses
is overflowing with the supernatural power of our Almighty
God. The Bible calls them miracles - unbelievable
happenings that we can't explain how or why it happened –
it just did. The miracle I find most amazing in the life of
Moses was the deliverance of God's people out of Egypt by
crossing the Red Sea. As Moses stretched out his hand over

the sea, it began to divide and the Israelites were able to cross over on dry land with towering high walls of water to their left and right. This is truly an example that ***nothing is impossible with God!*** Do you believe in miracles?

I want to stir you today to meditate on the wonder, working power of God. As a believer, that same power lives in you and is working in your life. God is in control and He can part the sea in your situation. He can do the impossible. There will be times in the adoption process when you will need to engage radical faith like Moses in order to release the captives and the orphans who are oppressed. Remember we have a real adversary in this process. Satan does not want to see the orphans delivered out of their oppressed situation. The Israelites were in captivity; but through Moses, God was able to deliver them to the promise land. Through *your* radical faith in God, you will bring an orphan child to their forever home. There will be days when you need to get radical, and not only ask God, but believe God, to move mightily in your adoption. Our daughter was expected to arrive in October; but, it was December and our new estimated time was late January or February. The movie stirred me to believe God for a miracle in my situation. Right in the middle of the theatre, tears flowing, my heart bursting with the mightiness of God in the impossible, I asked God to part my Red Sea and make a way for Makala to come home sooner than what we were told. Raise your staff, take a step of faith into the Red Sea, and believe God to make a way where there seems to be no way.

Baby Steps of Faith Personal Reflection

Exodus 14:16, 18   Raise your staff and stretch out your hand over the sea to divide the water so that the Israelites can go through…they will know that I am Lord.

Baby Step 66 – When did you last raise your staff?

Share your Story:

_____

_____

_____

_____

Trial or triumph? _____

Explain:

_____

_____

_____

_____

Personal Action Steps to Grow:

_____

_____

_____

_____

Supplication:

_____

_____

_____

_____

Genesis 35:11 And God said to Him, "I am God
Almighty…"

Jehovah – God of revelation; Jehovah-jireh – God our
provider; Jehovah-rophe – God our healer…God has many
names. Today, God would become our all sufficient, all
bountiful One, Mighty Promisor, giver of gifts – El-shaddai.
While Kyle and I were getting inspired about the miracles of
God at the Prince of Egypt movie, Kurt received news on the
homefront that our Red Sea was parting. Our caseworker
had called to tell us that our daughter was coming home – in
24 hours! Makala Myung Ok Han was preparing for travel to
America and her arrival was scheduled for December 31,
1998.

Kurt had planned to meet us at the theatre later that day to
grab some dinner and buy a new big screen television,
because that particular Christmas gift on his list didn't make
it under the tree. Little did Kyle and I know that Daddy
would arrive with such long awaited news. I am still amazed
at the details of that day. Hopeful that God would part our
Red Sea and make a way, Kyle and I made our way to the
theatre exit doors and walked into a winter wonderland of
fresh snow. The flakes were coming down…big, wet, frosty
snowflakes. The new fallen snow seemed to add wonder and
beauty to the moment. It was awe-inspiring for me…pure
fun for Kyle. Quickly, we jumped into the van and decided
to drive around the parking lot to see if we could find Dad.
No cell phones then, imagine that? It didn't take long to find
Kurt's truck on the lot. It's not every day you see someone

standing on the back of a pick-up, holding a huge poster sign in the middle of a heavy snow storm. There was something written on the poster board, but the snow was coming down heavy and it was hard to read. I couldn't help but think to myself, "Has the man gone mad? What on earth is he doing on the back of his truck? As we drove closer, the words on the poster were clear as ever, "Kyle are you ready to be a BIG BROTHER?"

El-Shaddai, The Lord God Almighty - The Mighty Promiser, the giver of gifts, the one who parts the sea, had made a way where there seemed to be no way.

Baby Steps of Faith Personal Reflection

Genesis 35:11 And God said to Him, "I am God
Almighty…"

*Baby Step 67 – Refer to the list. What Name of God
stirs your faith today?*

Share your Story:

_____
_____
_____
_____

Trial or triumph? _____

Explain:

_____
_____
_____
_____

Personal Action Steps to Grow:

_____
_____
_____
_____

Supplication:

_____
_____
_____
_____

THE OLD TESTAMENT NAMES OF GOD

Names are important to us and have meaning. I hope you like your name. Do you know what it means? What attributes or character qualities does a person with your name portray? With internet capability, finding this information is quick and simple. Your adopted child's name will be equally as important and I'm certain you'll take great care in selecting it. Names have personal connection. They are a unique part of us. Names in Biblical times were also very important. They revealed a person's character. As you read through scriptures you will see the importance of names. Take time to learn the **NAMES OF GOD.** God has many Names and each reveals Him in a different way. God's Names represent His attributes, His nature. I hope you are encouraged as you read the Names of God. Call upon God using the specific Name that connects Him with your situation. Allow the meaning of that particular Name of God to lift your faith. God is all these Names…all these things…and He loves us. O Lord, how excellent is Your Name in all the earth… (Psalm 8:1)

THE OLD TESTAMENT NAMES OF GOD

El Shaddai – Lord God Almighty
God of the mountains and mighty

El Elyon – The Most High – God
Sovereign over all – in control of all things

Adonai – Lord, Master
God's Leadership in our life

Yahweh – Lord, Jehovah
God's divine salvation for us

Jehovah Nissi – The Lord My Banner
God going before us

Jehovah- Raah – The Lord My Shepherd
God's friendship

Jehovah Rapha – The Lord That Heals
God's healing for us

Jehovah Shammah – The Lord is There
God is with us – present

Jehovah Tsidkenu – The Lord Our Righteousness
God's righteousness for us

Jehovah Mekoddishkem – The Lord Who Sanctifies You
God who makes us holy

El Olam – The Everlasting God
The God of eternity

Elohim – God
The God of power and might

Quanna – Jealous
God wants us to worship Him only

Jehovah Jireh – The Lord Will Provide
God who meets our needs

Jehovah Shalom – The Lord Is Peace
God who gives peace

Jehovah Sabaoth – The Lord of Hosts
God over all of heaven and earth

1 Thessalonians 5:24 The One who calls you is faithful
and He will do it.

Our adoption journey started through a painful event – a
complete unexpected hysterectomy. Your decision to adopt
may have been birthed out of a similar agonizing barren
place; for others, it may have been prompted by a heartfelt
desire to fulfill God's command, exercise compassion, and
care for the orphans. The scriptures tell us how God cares for
the weak and vulnerable, the fatherless. God called us all to
adoption and we answered, "yes," but He is ultimately the
One who will do it. He is faithful to finish the work He
started and bring families together one child at a time to
their forever homes.

In our sudden move of God, we found ourselves joyfully
preparing to travel. God had parted our Red Sea and made a
way. Our daughter arrived in Chicago, through a Korean
escort service, just twenty-four hours after we received the
caseworker's call. We were absolutely amazed at the
goodness of the Lord and His mighty power. I remember
asking the caseworker how this was possible, that our
daughter would be arriving in the United States December
31, 1998, while the Korean government offices remained
closed till January 1. She replied, "I have no idea...it's an
impossible scenario, even if personnel came into the office
days early, there's a great deal of paperwork to process and
travel arrangements to be made. It usually takes 4-6
weeks...but, I have a fax that states otherwise, so PRAISE
GOD and pack your bags!"

Miracles are happenings that we are unable to explain how or why it happened, but it did because the One who calls you is faithful and He will do it. Jesus tells us to have faith and not doubt His power. We serve a mountain moving God – the God of the impossible. Our precious daughter from South Korea would make a long journey from – Seoul, Korea – Tokyo, Japan – Detroit, Michigan – Chicago, Illinois – St. Louis, Missouri – to her forever home in Trenton, Illinois. It was happening. Makala Myung Kohlbrecher would arrive the last day of the year. It just seems fitting to say…*thus saith the Lord!*

Baby Steps of Faith Personal Reflection

1 Thessalonians 5:24 The One who calls you is faithful
and He will do it.

Baby Step 68 – Do you need a sudden move of God?

Share your Story:

_____
_____
_____
_____

Trial or triumph? _____

Explain:

_____
_____
_____
_____

Personal Action Steps to Grow:

_____
_____
_____
_____

Supplication:

_____
_____
_____
_____

1 Corinthians 2:9 No eye has seen, no ear has heard,
no mind has conceived what God has prepared for
those who love Him.

1 Corinthians 2:9 is my husband's favorite bible verse. These
words would become all the more real to me as I prepared to
meet Makala for the first time. Although our journey started
in 1994, God had this life event planned a long time ago. No
mind has conceived, no eye has seen, no ear has heard that
which God has planned for us and for you. It's hard to
describe the overwhelming feeling of joy and completeness
that comes in meeting your child for the first time. After so
much longing in our hearts, work, struggle, and waiting, the
placement is momentous. You've spent lots of time
preparing for this first meeting with your child and his/her
placement to your home. You have completed every facet of
the adoption process and endured the wait. You've prepared
a room, purchased clothes, found small tokens to decorate
and personalized their nurseries/rooms, found the favorite
blanket, and perhaps, a soft, cuddly stuffed animal or two.
Since receiving Makala's photo in July, this had become our
family declaration, "We have named her and claimed her
and called her our own; now it's time to bring her home!"

We were extremely excited and nervous at the same time.
How would she look at eight months of age? She was two
months old in her referral photo, surely she's grown and
changed. Would she be happy? Smiling? Cooing? Would she
cry when she saw us? I was horrified that she wouldn't want
me to hold or cuddle her. I tried not to set my expectations
high. Our training had prepared us for this moment and we

were aware that the happiest adopting parents are those that understand their dream child, may not being so dreamy, and the perfect first time meeting, may not go perfect at all.

Your child descends from different ancestors and circumstances. If adopting international, your child comes from a different culture – and all the familiar sights, sounds, and scents of their surroundings have changed instantly. Some adopted children have survived conditions most of us have never seen. You may be asked to provide the child's going-home clothes and shoes, because your adopted child must leave their clothes behind for another orphan. You may be given specific directions on what and how to feed your child the first few days or longer in order to adjust to different foods or the fact that it's plentiful now. You may see your child for the first time at the adoption agency abroad, a foster home, hotel or an airport like us. The location can have an impact on the first meeting. Airports are noisy! Your first meeting is a joyous occasion; but it can be superimposed with thoughts of the birth parents' grief. I recall tearful moments as I reflected on Woo Ree Han and what she might be feeling or going through at this time in her life.

One by one, the passengers exited the plane; but, only one Korean escort. We knew it was her immediately. Makala had grown so much since her photo. Her rosy cheeks and ready smile will be cinematically recorded in my memory forever. We all held her close, laughed, and cried tears of joy. Kyle was so excited to finally have his little sister. People congratulated us in the airport and commented how "lucky" she was to be adopted. However, we realized that we were the ones who were so incredibly blessed and enriched. No eye has seen, no ear has heard, no mind has conceived what God has prepared for those who love Him.

Baby Steps of Faith Personal Reflection

1 Corinthians 2:9 No eye has seen, no ear has heard, no mind has conceived what God has prepared for those who love Him.

Baby Step 69 – How are you preparing to meet your child for the first time?

Share your Story:

_____
_____
_____
_____

Trial or triumph? _____

Explain:

_____
_____
_____
_____

Personal Action Steps to Grow:

_____
_____
_____
_____

Supplication:

_____
_____
_____
_____

Psalm 107:8 Let them give thanks to the LORD for his
unfailing love and his wonderful deeds for men, for
he satisfies the thirsty and fills the hungry
with good things.

Happy New Year! Makala may not have been here for
Christmas, but she knew how to ring in the New Year. We
managed to make a whirlwind trip to Chicago airport to
pick up our baby from South Korea and be home in time to
ring in the new year – Welcome 1999. "Let them give thanks
to the LORD for his unfailing love and His wonderful
deeds…" That's exactly what we purposed to do in sharing
Makala's arrival news with everyone in the family. Our trip
was last minute, with a quick turn around time, so we
decided to keep it a secret and once again let our creative
flare take over as we planned the perfect way to introduce
the newest member to the family! Let the *Arrival Day
Celebration* begin!

The first honorary visit was the grandparents. It was a cold,
snowy night and we were bundled up like Eskimos. Hiding
a tiny infant in a blanket was not a difficult task, but to
insure the element of surprise Kurt and I trailed behind
Kyle's grand entrance and snuck into another room. Without
hesitation, Kyle ran into the living room where Grandma
was enjoying her recliner and he handed her Makala's
passport. "Kyle, where did you get this? Is this Makala's
passport? Did you get your baby sister?" Kyle refrained
from replying and waited patiently for the grand entrance of
his new baby sister. More emphatically and excited

Grandma insisted that Kyle give her an answer. It was time to interrupt this inquisition and introduce the new granddaughter. Grandma began to shout up the stairs for Grandpa and within seconds, sounds of great celebration filled the air. Over the next few days, Makala would meet more and more of her new family. She would receive what God had intended - love, acceptance, and a place of belonging. I would find these things as well.

For years, I wandered in the wasteland restless, uncertain, hungry and thirsty for answers in my childlessness, suffering in this inner famine. God heard my cries and during the adoption journey, He gradually set me free to a place of excitement and security. He quenched my thirst and filled my empty soul. I cried out to the Lord in my trouble, and he delivered me from my distress. He led me by a straight way. (Paraphrased Psalm 107: 6-7) I would discover His unfailing love and receive His wonderful deeds. God truly does satisfy us and fills our lives with good things. Be wise to observe what God has done in your life and in your adoption process. I pray that you will have a personal understanding and a deep appreciation for the His loving kindness. Happy Arrival Day – Happy New You – Praise the Lord for His goodness!

Baby Steps of Faith Personal Reflection

Psalm 107:8 Let them give thanks to the LORD for his
unfailing love and his wonderful deeds for men, for
he satisfies the thirsty and fills the hungry
with good things.

Baby Step 70 – How are you planning to celebrate your child's arrival day?

Share your Story:

_____
_____
_____
_____

Trial or triumph? _____

Explain:

_____
_____
_____
_____

Personal Action Steps to Grow:

_____
_____
_____
_____

Supplication:

_____
_____
_____
_____

James 1:17 Every good and perfect gift is from above,
coming down from the Father…

Makala's arrival celebration continued on New Year's Day
as we visited aunts, uncles, and cousins. Although the
grandparents were surprised the night before, they kept our
secret until we could visit everyone on New Year's. Just
hours after we arrived home from the airport, a cold front
came through and brought a winter clipper. We woke up to
six inches of fresh snow on the ground; but, it wasn't enough
to keep us from introducing the newest member of the
family – Makala Myung. Today would be a day of surprises!

Now, I'm fairly sure you know what a surprise is; but,
humor me in sharing the definition – a surprise is anything
that happens *that you don't see coming.* Surprises are
enjoyable, like a surprise birthday party or a baby
announcement as in this case. Some surprises can be
annoying and devastating – like the loss of a job or a
negative doctor report. Our God is the God of great
surprises. Mary the virgin would find herself pregnant with
the Savior of the World. It's safe to say, no one saw that
coming. Jesus was a king born in a stable in
Bethlehem…surprise. God knows how to surprise His
people and I can assure you, that in the middle of every
situation in life, He finds a way to remind us of His
presence, great love, and encouragement. We wanted to
encourage and remind the family of God's great love and
provision. They endured with us, hoped and prayed for us,
and it was time to introduce the perfect gift from above.

This time we would surprise everyone with more than a photograph. We took a large over-sized box and cut out one side of it, gift wrapped it, and placed a huge bow on the front. Makala snuggled quietly across my chest in her baby carrier. This freed my hands to hold the gift box over her and successfully pull off the surprise. Kyle would ring doorbells and naturally family and friends would answer the door and find the Kohlbrecher's. Keeping with the fun, we explained our desire to give them a gift for New Year's. It was quite entertaining to watch each one take the box from my hands and reveal the newest member of the family. Shock and awe would best describe the moments that transpired after each unveiling.

We will always treasure that snowy New Year's Day. Get ready to surprise family and friends when your child comes home. Plan the fun in advance and be creative. There are too few surprises in life, strive to make his/her first appearance a memorable one for family, friends, and yourselves. Every good and perfect gift comes from the Father – enjoy the element of surprise.

Baby Steps of Faith Personal Reflection

James 1:17 Every good and perfect gift is from above,
coming down from the Father...

*Baby Step 71 – Was your most recent adoption
surprise enjoyable or annoying?*

Share your Story:

_____

_____

_____

_____

Trial or triumph? _____

Explain:

_____

_____

_____

_____

Personal Action Steps to Grow:

_____

_____

_____

_____

Supplication:

_____

_____

_____

_____

Hebrews 13:8 Jesus Christ is the same yesterday and
today and forever.

Just a few months after Makala arrived home, she turned a
year old. Each day I find myself more attached to this
precious child. I continue to make new discoveries about our
daughter. There have been lots of changes to my household
since the addition of a baby…it happens…consider yourself
warned. Getting up several times during the night, bottle
feedings, and *changing* diapers are all part of the parenting
package.

Some days I look back at my journal notes and all that has
transpired over the last five years and I am amazed how
clearly I can trace God's hand *now.* It's true what they say
about hindsight. It does give you 20/20 vision. I've also gone
through lots of *changes* over the years – physically, mentally,
emotionally, and spiritually on this adoption journey. As
time moves on, we move along with it. We are constantly
changing and so are the situations in our lives. The good
news is Jesus doesn't change. Jesus is the same yesterday,
today, and tomorrow. He is always there for us through
every season of change in our lives.

Makala received two gifts that illustrates beautifully the
constant, all-knowing, faithful God we serve. The first one
was a beautiful Korean girl figurine. Makala's Grandma
received this gift forty years ago by a family member who
had fought in the Korean War. It was a keepsake and tucked
away. Little did anyone know all those years ago, that it

would have such profound significance, and one day become a gift for her Korean granddaughter.

The second gift was a baby doll. The grandparents had searched everywhere for a baby doll. That doesn't seem like such a tall order, but they wanted it to be an Asian doll. That's a different story when you live in America, but they found one. As I admired the doll, I noticed something attached to her garment. It was a small booklet inserted in a plastic holder. I was immediately drawn to it, because it had a huge rainbow on the front and the word passport. I gently pulled it from the plastic sleeve and opened it. This little booklet shared the salvation message of Jesus Christ. The one constant in life is Jesus. He is dependable. You can always count on Jesus' unchanging love, devotion, and concern for every detail of your life in every season and circumstance. He is the same yesterday and today and tomorrow.

Baby Steps of Faith Personal Reflection

Hebrews 13:8 Jesus Christ is the same yesterday and today and forever.

Baby Step 72 – What is constant about Jesus in your life of changes and seasons?

Share your Story:

_____

_____

_____

_____

Trial or triumph? _____

Explain:

_____

_____

_____

_____

Personal Action Steps to Grow:

_____

_____

_____

_____

Supplication:

_____

_____

_____

_____

Psalm 48:14 For this God is our God for ever and ever;
he will be our guide even to the end.

God revealed Himself to us so many times during our
adoption journey. We are still amazed at how he continues
to show us each day that Makala was purposed and planned
for us. I want to encourage you that His adoption plan for
you is just as absolute. It's meant to be my friend. I love that
God continues to bless our adoption and touch our lives in
the most personal ways. Most recently, it was through a
keepsake painting. My husband and I love to collect Jesse
Barnes paintings. We have several hanging in our home.
When Kyle was born, we chose a painting especially for him
as a keepsake. The painting is called "Starlight in
December." It seemed fitting since Kyle was born in
December. The painting depicts a snowy small town scene.
It's a peaceful night. The moon and stars shine bright on the
new fallen snow. The homes on this quiet street continue to
convey this tranquil scene. As you peer into the windows,
you find crackling fireplaces, stockings on the mantle, and
beautifully lit Christmas trees. It's the perfect keepsake for
our son who was born in December.

I mentioned to my husband that we should begin our search
for Makala's keepsake painting. As we discussed hitting a
gallery or two, we began to recall a painting that we had
purchased many years ago. Where was that painting? What
closet was it hiding in? Better yet, what did it look like? It
was in a tube – that much we remembered. The search began
and the mystery painting was found. As we pulled the

portrait from the tube and gently unrolled it on the table, I could hardly believe my eyes. How could a painting purchased years ago, long before infertility and the adoption process, speak so profoundly to us today? Because we serve a God who knows the plan – who has a purpose for us – and guides us to the very end. The painting is a beautiful portrait of a little church in the woods. The scene is evening and a rain storm has passed, evident of the dark clouds in the distance. Amidst the breaking sky is a beautiful rainbow, the sign of God's faithfulness. At the bottom of the print, etched in our minds and hearts forever, is the print title...the precious words that sealed the rainbow covenant – *God's Promise.* Psalm 48:14 For this God is our God forever and ever, He will be our guide even to the end.

Baby Steps of Faith Personal Reflection

Psalm 48:14 For this God is our God for ever and ever;
he will be our guide even to the end.

*Baby Step 73 – Describe and title your adoption
keepsake portrait?*

Share your Story:

_____
_____
_____
_____

Trial or triumph? _____

Explain:

_____
_____
_____
_____

Personal Action Steps to Grow:

_____
_____
_____
_____

Supplication:

_____
_____
_____
_____

Jeremiah 29:11 "For I know the plans I have for you,"
declares the LORD – "plans to give you
hope and a future."

The following excerpt was the last to be penned in my
adoption journal. I was officially a mother of two young
children, wife, and a teacher. Apparently, I no longer had
time to journal! Not true, I still enjoy taking good sermon
notes and journaling scriptural reflections. I hope that
you've been diligent to pen your personal adoption
experiences. These noted milestones will become invaluable
to you and serve as a treasured memoir for your adopted
child.

Mother's Day 1999 – Makala is so beautiful and has brought
us so much joy. We have survived late night feedings and
the family is back to a normal sleeping pattern. Kyle can't
seem to get enough of his little sister. A few days ago, Kurt
started "fishing" for Mother's Day gift ideas. Jokingly, I told
him that it had to be something really big this year, because I
labored extra long and hard for this second child. For my
first Mother's Day, I received a beautiful ring. Again, I
dropped subtle hints for a second piece of jewelry – it's a
weakness. My husband asked to see the ring I received
seven years ago for my first Mother's Day. It was beautiful –
wide gold band and a gorgeous light sapphire stone in the
center. It's the December birthstone for Kyle. It was

surrounded by brilliant diamonds. As we observed the ring, we wondered what stone represented the month of April – Makala's birth month. As fate would have it, diamonds are the April birthstone. Some might call it coincidence; but I call it providence – the foreseeing care and guidance of God.

What a comfort to know He cares about the days, months, and years ahead of us. He cares about your future. Without a doubt, God knows the plans He has for you and it includes Mother's Day. Hold on to the promise, no matter where you're at in the process. Your rewards will be great – a deeper relationship with God, newfound freedom as you learn to live and walk like Christ, the promise of a child fulfilled, and that annual Mother's Day gift. It's a bonus! Keep taking those **Baby Steps of Faith** that will ultimately lead you to every day being a mother's day!

Baby Steps of Faith Personal Reflection

Jeremiah 29:11 "For I know the plans I have for you,"
declares the LORD – "plans to give you
hope and a future."

Baby Step 74 – Are you celebrating Mother's Day yet?

Share your Story:

_____
_____
_____
_____

Trial or triumph? _____

Explain:

_____
_____
_____
_____

Personal Action Steps to Grow:

_____
_____
_____
_____

Supplication:

_____
_____
_____
_____

ABOUT THE AUTHOR

Brenda Martin Kohlbrecher is a former school teacher with a desire to demonstrate and communicate this lesson: Faith + Adoption = Family She is passionate about all three parts of the adoption equation and is also an avid speaker, worship leader, and dramatist. In 1998 – Brenda, her husband Kurt, and biological son, Kyle, unanimously voted to adopt Makala from South Korea. Today, the Kohlbrecher family resides in Trenton, Illinois and their hearts remain steadfast towards adoption.

www.ingramcontent.com/pod-product-compliance
Lightning Source LLC
LaVergne TN
LVHW051228080426
835513LV00016B/1474